D0556826

MEDITATIONS ON THE CATHOLIC PRIESTHOOD

MEDITATIONS
ON THE
CATHOLIC PRIESTHOOD

Rev. Charles P. Connor, Ph.D.

ST PAULS

Alba House

Library of Congress Cataloging-in-Publication Data

Connor, Charles P. (Charles Patrick)
  Meditations on the Catholic priesthood / Charles P. Connor.
    p. cm.
  Includes bibliographical references.
  ISBN 0-8189-0976-5
1. Pastoral theology—Catholic Church—Meditations.   I. Title.

  BX1913.C635 2005
  262'.142—dc22

                          2004025164

Produced and designed in the United States of America by the
Fathers and Brothers of the Society of St. Paul,
2187 Victory Boulevard, Staten Island, New York 10314-6603,
as part of their communications apostolate.

ISBN: 0-8189-0976-5

Printing Information:

Current Printing - first digit   1   2   3   4   5   6   7   8   9   10

Year of Current Printing - first year shown

2005   2006   2007   2008   2009   2010   2011   2012   2013

Table of Contents

Foreword

Father Charles Connor has written a little book worth reading and re-reading by every American priest.

Vatican II reminds us that, "it is the liturgy through which, especially in the divine sacrifice of the Eucharist, 'the work of our redemption is accomplished'" (SC, 2). The Eucharist is the source and summit of our life as Christians. There is no Church without the Eucharist, and no Eucharist without the priest.

At the same time, throughout his long ministry, Pope John Paul II has urged priests again and again to take up the task of a "new evangelization" of the world. That work belongs to every Catholic, but especially to those of us who are priests. Vatican II says that, "…since nobody can be saved who has not first believed, it is the first task of priests as coworkers of bishops to preach the Gospel of God to all" (PO, 4). Our job as priests is converting the world.

Seeking an armistice with the spirit of the world, both outside us and within us, is an illusion. The Church in America faces an absolutely new and absolutely real kind of mission territory every day now, with all sorts of intractable pastoral challenges. We're a nation of rapidly growing cities, wealth, sophisticated media and excellent universities. We're also a nation of farms and ranches, huge distances, the unemployed, undocumented immigrants, the homeless and the poor.

We're blessed with a thriving Hispanic population who are naturally drawn to the Catholic faith, but we're also hobbled by a lack of personnel and resources to serve these thousands of good people as they need.

We live in a nation of great material success and scientific self-assurance, but where the inner life is withering away, where private spiritualities replace communities of real faith, and where loneliness is now the daily routine of millions of people. Every priest knows this just from the confessions we hear in a year.

America is mission territory—whether we recognize it yet or not; whether we do our ministry in Pittsburgh, Fargo, Los Angeles, Miami or Denver—and we need a new Pentecost. We need to be priests who are men of prayer, men of courage, men for others, men anchored in the sacramental life of the Church. We need to be priests who will spark not a new clericalism, but a new friendship, new equality, new cooperation and *new fire* from every vocation and form of discipleship in the Church.

We need to be priests who can answer generously and honestly *yes* when Jesus asks us, "Simon, son of John, *do you love me?*" (Jn 21:15).

God is calling us to be those priests right now. He's calling us to be what He saw in our hearts when He first spoke our names. And so the prayer we need to keep on our lips, as we look to the hopes and difficulties that lie ahead, is "thank you"— *thank you God* for delivering me from myself; *thank you God* for calling me to your service; *thank you God* for demanding from me a life of holiness; *thank you God* for giving me the brother priests who support me on the way.

In that spirit, as a priest and bishop, I've found Father Connor's words here to be a source of encouragement, clarity and renewal. May these pages lead other brothers to more deeply treasure the heart of their priesthood, and to renew their zeal for Jesus Christ.

✠ *Charles J. Chaput, O.F.M. Cap.*
Archbishop of Denver

Introduction

About ten years ago, while I was attending a week of spiritual and pastoral renewal of a group of diocesan priests, I was privileged to listen to a gifted theologian, a layman, give a presentation on the priest as "Icon of Christ." The phraseology was borrowed from the post-Synodal Exhortation on the Priesthood, *Pastores Dabo Vobis*. Our Holy Father, Pope John Paul II, gave the priests of the contemporary world a great gift when he published *Pastores Dabo Vobis* in 1992. The Exhortation was based on suggestions given to the Holy Father by Bishops who met in a Synod in 1990, but clearly the document is an expression of the Pope's own heart and mind on the nature of the Priesthood. Anyone who is a student of the papacy of Pope John Paul II knows that one of the strongest themes in his teaching is a desire for the members of the Church to know, understand, and live the authentic teachings of the Second Vatican Council. The Pope's desire to keep aloft the teachings of the Council is especially true in regard to that assembly's teachings about the Priesthood. The Council made it very plain that the priest is not merely a functionary, not simply an elected Church official. At ordination, a priest is changed at the very level of his being. He becomes another person, more configured than ever to the Person of Christ, commissioned not simply to act in the name of Christ, but to be another Christ, an *alter Christus*. This teaching was not an original insight of the Second Vatican Council. It is the traditional teaching of the Church. However, the Fathers of the Second Vatican Council, surveying the state of the priesthood in the mid-twentieth century, saw immediately that they had to express once again, in fresh terms, the essence of the priesthood.

At the week of renewal to which I referred above, I soon learned, perhaps in a harsh way, how very timely were the Council's teachings about the priesthood and how relevant was the Holy Father's issuance of *Pastores Dabo Vobis.* After the lecturer gave a magnificent explanation about the manner in which an icon is a window to the divine and how in an analogous sense an ordained priest, being an *alter Christus*, is a window to heavenly realities in and through Jesus Christ, the vast majority of the priests were deeply moved by the speech. However, one priest reacted quite angrily. He said that he had hoped for a presentation which would help priests with their psychological needs. The priest indicated that he did not have much interest in hearing about the priest being an icon of Christ. He wanted psychological reinforcement to handle better his daily priestly activities.

I was astounded at this outburst. How could anyone dismiss the beautiful, indeed humbling, doctrine that mere men are raised above themselves to be other Christs, and therefore to do things for their fellow Christians which they could never do solely on the basis of their own weak humanity? Then I began to realize that the priest's angry words were an indication of a vast lack of knowledge about the nature of the priesthood. While this priest was mostly alone in expressing his irritation with the talk, I could tell that other priests present hesitated in accepting fully the fact that they were configured ontologically as other Christs. They had no objection to the doctrine, but it was not concrete enough for them, the way a psychological presentation might have been. Furthermore, the Council's doctrine on the sacramental character of Holy Orders and the way it configures a priest to the Person of Jesus Christ, Head and Chief Shepherd of the Church, has been heard rather rarely in comparison to books and lectures about the morale and psychological state of contemporary priests. I must admit that over the years, I have found few priests who have reacted as angrily as the priest I just described, but I have met far too many who react with a lack of deep understanding of the doctrine presented in *Pastores Dabo Vobis*. Since they do not properly understand "who" they are (i.e., new persons in Christ) as a result of Holy Orders, they do not know sufficiently "what" to do in their daily priestly activity. Thus disabled, they may bump along in their years of priestly service without any deep crises, but more likely they will soon become disoriented. Temptations, distractions, and sometimes addictions displace the sense of union with Christ which He intended them to have. Alienation sets in. No wonder so many priests have abandoned the active ministry in recent decades. No wonder that only a diminished number of young men respond positively to Christ's sure and constant call for them to become priestly workers in the vineyard of the Church.

Several years ago, I heard a priest lament that there were no writers around today who could write in a "meat and potatoes" way about the teachings of the Church. The priest was referring to the Chestertons and the Sheeds of past years. I sincerely hope that this priest will have a chance to read Father Charles Connor's present book, *Meditations on the Catholic Priesthood*. In Father Connor, he will find a latter-day Chesterton or Sheed taking the beautiful and challenging teachings on the priesthood of the Second Vatican Council and of Pope John Paul II, and making them truly "meat and potatoes." I must admit that though I had the best of theological formations in my seminary years, I was moved to new insights by many passages in Father Connor's book.

In the early chapters of his book, Father Connor, a distinguished church historian, who has inspired a wide audience with his books and lectures, presents a historical survey of the Church's teachings on the priesthood. Naturally, he starts with Sacred Scripture, moves on to the Fathers of the Church, and shows how the Church has responded to various crises about the nature of the priesthood, especially during the Reformation. Father Connor shows himself not only to be a good historian, but also a good theologian. He presents the Church's challenging teachings about the priesthood in simple, yet compelling terms. Having placed the reader on a firm footing of understanding about the priesthood, Father Connor then moves on to address certain themes, like the relationship between the priesthood and the Holy Eucharist. Our Holy Father constantly and correctly insists that without the priesthood, there can be no Eucharist; without the Eucharist, there can be no Church. I believe that someday authors will comment not only on the contributions of Pope John Paul II to the theology of the body and to sacramental theology, but also to ecclesiology, with his constant connecting of priesthood, Eucharist, and Church. Father Connor helps the priest to see in the Eucharist his *raison d'être* for being a priest, the source of all his strength in the ministry, the summit of all his prayers. I can only expect that greater pastoral zeal will come about in our midst as priests see better through Father Connor's book the connection between their daily Eucharist and the pastoral charity which they must subsequently exercise.

As Father Connor's book assists priests to become more deeply immersed in an authentic understanding of their priestly identity, they will become more and more identified with Christ the Victim. In my opinion, Father Connor's chapter on the role of the Cross and suffering in the life of a priest is one of the highlights of this book. So many priests (and Bishops!) today seem scandalized at their heavy burdens and the nature of their pastoral challenges. If Christ suffered, not only on the Cross but throughout his earthly existence, can the priest really expect to be like Christ, to be an *alter Christus*, and then glide through life? Yet, the suffering of a priest is tinged with joy, because he suffers along with Christ, bolstered by Jesus Himself. I believe that many priests will have their courage restored if they can only know how precious they are to Christ the Priest and Victim. Father Connor's book will be particularly helpful here.

One of the great priestly challenges is the commitment to celibacy. This is a particular way of living with Christ the Victim. In characteristic fashion, Father Connor connects the priest's commitment to celibacy to the Person of Christ. If the priest is another Christ, why not live fully the way Christ did, celibate, single-hearted, devoted completely to God and His people? Once again, if priests perceive of themselves solely as hired hands, they might naturally cringe at the thought of celibacy. But if the priest concentrates on his identity with Jesus, the Chaste One, the Poor One, and the Obedient One, celibacy makes complete sense. It is not at all an impossible ideal, but a form of communion with Christ.

After surveying other themes, notably the specific contribution of Pope John Paul II to a renewed understanding of the Church's teachings on the ministry and life of priests, Father Connor closes with a magnificent chapter about the priest and his relationship with Mary, Mother of Jesus Christ. Since the priest enjoys a unique relationship with Christ, as Father Connor reminds us, then he enjoys a unique relationship with the Blessed Mother. She loves priests no less than she loved her Son. How very moving it is to know that we have Mary's special help as we seek to live in priestly fidelity.

I recommend Father Connor's book wholeheartedly and with joy. It is my sincere hope that all priests will be encouraged, that suffering priests will be refreshed, and that young men aspiring to the priesthood will advance with greater commitment to the priesthood as a result of this excellent work. I thank Father Connor not only for giving to priests a renewed priestly joy, but to me, his Bishop, a deeper gratitude to Jesus Christ for my own priestly and episcopal identity.

Most Rev. Joseph F. Martino, D.D., Hist. E.D.
Bishop of Scranton

MEDITATIONS ON THE CATHOLIC PRIESTHOOD

1

What Is the Priesthood?

This work is not intended to be a commentary on contemporary crises affecting the Catholic priesthood. Nor is it a study on declining numbers of vocations in the twenty-first century. Rather, it is a meditation on the timeless truths of Holy Orders. As such, one must begin by answering the question: What is a priest? The dictionary responds succinctly: One whose office is to perform religious rites, and especially to make sacrificial offerings.

The roots of the Catholic priesthood go back to Judaism in their historical development, and in that development we find two forms of the reality of the priesthood: the exercise of priestly functions and an emphasis on priestly holiness. A sacrificial liturgical offering is to be found in the earliest patriarchal society, usually performed by the heads of families. Moses has never been considered a member of the priestly caste, yet in the book of Exodus we read:

> Moses came and told the people all the words of the Lord, all his laws. The whole people answered with one voice and said, "We will do all that the Lord has told us." Moses wrote down all the words of the Lord. He rose early in the morning and built an altar at the foot of the mountain, and put up twelve sacred pillars,

one for each of the twelve tribes of Israel. He then sent the young men of Israel and they sacrificed bulls to the Lord as whole offerings and shared offerings. Moses took half the blood and put it in basins and the other half he flung against the altar. Then he took the book of the covenant and read it aloud for all the people to hear. They said, "We will obey, and do all that the Lord has said." Moses then took the blood and flung it over the people, saying, "This is the blood of the covenant which the Lord has made with you on the terms of this book."[1]

During the reign of Kings David and Solomon, they themselves, as monarchs, offered priestly sacrifices. Even more poignant was the sacrifice of Melchisedech, King of Salem. He is considered a type of Christ because of his combined kingship and priesthood, and because his offering of bread and wine is seen as foreshadowing the Eucharist.

Then Melchisedech, King of Salem, brought food and wine. He was priest of God Most High, and he pronounced this blessing on Abram: "Blessed be Abram by God Most High, creator of heaven and earth. And blessed be God Most High, who has delivered your enemies into your power."[2]

During the period of the Judges, we begin to speak of the Levitical priesthood. An hereditary priesthood was aided by Levites, descendants of the Jewish patriarch Levi. Such men were hereditary ministers to the Temple priests, and were at times joined by certain prophets who functioned in a cultic way. Hence, by now, there was a certain blending of the priestly and prophetic offices.

---

[1] Exodus 24:3-8.

[2] Genesis 14:18-20.

As the centuries progressed, Old Testament priests previously engaged in teaching, delivering divine oracles and handing down the law, had their functions replaced by wise men, scholars of the law and scribes. The priestly function became almost solely confined to worship, and the cultivation of a ritual purity of holiness, viewed as necessary for one who handled objects belonging to the Temple, and entered into the sacred precincts.

These Old Testament priests, whatever their function, ministered in some fashion to the People of God. Since the Second Vatican Council, there has been a renewed emphasis on the Church as the People of God, specifically to stress our spiritual heritage, our roots in Israel. We, as Catholics, believe there to be only one People of God, one Mystical Body of Christ: those who prepared for His coming in the Old Testament, those who lived during Our Lord's own earthly life, those who came after Him to our own time, and those who will live on this earth until the end of time. There is one mission shared in by this one People of God who have been redeemed by the blood of Christ, and for its universality there exists one common priesthood, that of Jesus Christ, the Eternal High Priest. While all the faithful are sharers in Christ's priesthood, the Second Vatican Council very clearly taught that certain members are called very specifically by Christ to be uniquely configured to Him in the ministerial priesthood, one which gives them a "*Sacra Potestas*," to share in the authority of Him who is Priest, Prophet and King.

The Council also reminded the faithful that the ministerial priesthood differs "in essence and degree" from their own participation. This difference is the result of a special gift of the Holy Spirit bestowed on a man in the sacrament of Holy Orders, enabling him to act "*in persona Christi*" as he offers the Eucharistic sacrifice and forgives sins. The highest degree of priesthood was conferred by Christ on His apostles and, through them, on their successors, the bishops.

These in their turn have legitimately handed on to different individuals in the Church various degrees of participation in the ministry ... although priests do not possess the highest degree of the priesthood, and although they are dependent on the bishops in the exercise of their power, they are nevertheless united with the bishops in sacerdotal dignity. By the power of the sacrament of Holy Orders, and in the image of Christ, the eternal High Priest, they are consecrated to preach the Gospel, shepherd the faithful, and celebrate divine worship as the priests of the New Testament.[3]

God, then, chooses certain men, endows them with supernatural gifts which, by their nature are mysterious, and empowers these men to go among their fellow members of Christ's body, transforming them with the sacramental life of grace. Because they are God's unique choice, they are not the product of a popular vote by their peers. At the same time, they are anything but superior to their peers; they work with the continuous assistance of all the faithful sharers in the common priesthood of Christ, and are always in need of their help, their encouragement and their prayers. This is so because, like their brothers and sisters, they are weak, fragile members of humanity who must offer sacrifices for their own sins, as well as those of the world.

For every high priest is taken from among men and appointed their representative before God, to offer gifts and sacrifices for sins. He is able to bear patiently with the ignorant and erring, since he, too, is beset by weakness, and because of this he is bound to make sin-offerings for himself no less than for the people. And nobody arrogates the honor to himself: he is called by God, as indeed Aaron was.[4]

---

[3] *Lumen Gentium* (Dogmatic Constitution on the Church) III:28, in Walter M. Abbott, S.J. (Ed.), *The Documents of Vatican II* (New York: Herder & Herder, 1966), 53.

[4] Hebrews 5:1-4.

Since it is God who has chosen him, it is God who will ultimately measure his success, and no priest may ever legitimately measure his success by earthly standards. He is a man sent to proclaim God's message, a message made incarnate in the person of God's only Son, and proclaimed through the Church which that same Son established. The message is to be proclaimed clearly and unambiguously in season and out of season, when popular and unpopular. One Bishop was fond of telling his Ordinands to enjoy the applause given at the ordination ceremony, and to savor it, especially at those moments in their priesthood when people would be severely castigating them for teaching what the Church teaches. In short, the priest does not tell the community what it wants to hear; he tells the truth Christ wants it to hear. To do so is simply part of being a priest, a point one seminary rector was quick to make in a conference to the seminarians under his charge:

> The Priesthood is a call, not a career; a redefinition of self, not just a new ministry; a way of life, not a job; a state of being, not just a function; a permanent, lifelong commitment, not a temporary style of service; an identity, not just a role. We are priests; yes the doing, the ministry, is mighty important, but it flows from the being; we can act like priests, minister as priests, function as priests, serve as priests, preach as priests, because first and foremost we are priests! Being before act![5]

The being of the priest, in philosophical terms, is described as the ontological change that has taken place in him with his reception of Holy Orders. This change underscores his consecration, as well as his total and complete dedication to the Church.

---

[5] Timothy M. Dolan, *Priests for the Third Millennium* (Huntington, IN: Our Sunday Visitor Press, 2000), 228.

Above all else, a priest is a consecrated man. There is a clear difference between a man as such and a Christian, for Baptism imposes on its recipients an indelible character, a permanent mark, so permanent and indelible that it can never be erased, and this makes him really and truly a man. There is also a difference between a Christian as such and a priest, for the sacrament of Holy Orders confers on the Christian who receives it a new character, a new mark which is also permanent and indelible, making its recipient a priest forever—a *sacerdos in aeternum*. Just as anyone who has been baptized is saved or damned as a Christian, so the Christian who has been ordained is saved or damned as a priest. He has taken an irreversible step that leaves him marked out forever.

When a Christian is ordained he receives and accepts something new that never disappears, something that changes him and makes him different from all others. God takes possession of him in a special way; He consecrates him to His service for the benefit of the rest of mankind, his brothers and sisters; He makes him a sharer in Christ's priesthood and gives him a new personality.... He is a priest continuously, internally, invisibly; he is a priest always and at every moment, whether he is performing the highest and most sublime office or the most vulgar and humble action of his ordinary life. Just as a Christian cannot leave aside the fact that he is a new man, that Baptism has given him a particular character, and act "as if" he were just a man purely and simply, neither can a priest leave aside his priestly character and behave "as if" he were not a priest....[6]

The reason a priest is always a priest, is because of his unique configuration to Christ, and this configuration is no-

---

[6] Federico Suarez, *About Being a Priest* (Princeton: Scepter Publishers, 1996), 8.

where better seen than in the priest's identification with the cross; a priest is never more a priest than when he is identified with the cross of Christ. Sharing in Christ's sufferings can be of many sorts; it might be the physical endurance of torture and incarceration, the spiritual struggle of perseverance in the face of doubt or temptation, or the transference of parishioners' sufferings to the life of the priest himself. The more pronounced the sign of the cross in the life of a priest, the more effective his priesthood is for those he is sent to serve, and the more effective it is for his own personal sanctification, for, as the English Benedictine writer, Dom Hubert Van Zeller, has observed, the priestly vocation has a twofold purpose, personal sanctification and the salvation of souls.

This identification with the cross has been called victimhood by many classical authors. Just as Christ was a priest and a victim on the altar of the cross, offering Himself to the Heavenly Father, and at the same time being offered, so the priest, configured to Christ the High Priest, is both offerer in the Holy Sacrifice of the Mass, and at the same time offered, a victim for others' salvation. For many years, both in his writing and preaching of priests' retreats, the late Archbishop Fulton J. Sheen developed this idea in great detail. He made the point that our Lord differed from all other priests—pagan and Jewish—because all other priests offered a victim distinct from themselves. a goat, a lamb, a bullock, etc., but Christ offered Himself as a victim. In the words of the Letter to the Hebrews, "He offered Himself without blemish to God, a spiritual and eternal sacrifice" (9:14). How Christ was both priest and victim, Sheen related in detail:

> As a victim He was identified with sinners: "God made Him one with the sinfulness of men, so that in Him we might be made one with the goodness of God Himself" (2 Corinthians 5:21).
> As a priest, He was holy with the holiness of God:
> As a victim, He was "made sin."

As a priest, He was "separated from the world."
As a victim, He came into it to fight against the Devil,
    the Prince of the world.
On the cross, He was upright as a priest;
On the cross, He was prostrate as a victim.
As priest, He mediated with the Father;
As victim, He mediated for the sins of men.
Before Pilate, He spoke seven times as
    the Priest-Shepherd;
Before Pilate, He was silent seven times as the Victim-Lamb.
As a priest He has vertical relations with heaven;
As a victim He has horizontal relations with earth.
As a priest He had dignity;
As a victim He suffered indignity.
As a priest: God is alive;
As a victim: God is dead.
As a priest He prays to the Father that the Cup pass;
As a victim He drinks it to its dregs....[7]

Archbishop Sheen noted that since the priest was configured to Christ, his life bore the resemblance of the cross: vertically, he was related to the Eternal High Priest in heaven; horizontally, he was related to all humanity. Vertically, his vocation derived from Christ. All the effectiveness of his priesthood came from Christ, all the sacraments he administered, the truths he preached, the vocations he fostered, the supernatural works he performed, had nothing to do with him as an individual, they flowed from the One who gave him his priesthood. Horizontally, the priest resembled the Christ who had assumed a human nature. Just as Christ took upon Himself our infirmities and bore our ills, so priests were representative of sinful humanity.

    The priest's configuration to Christ, priest and victim, is seen most forcefully in the Holy Sacrifice of the Mass, the paschal mystery given us by Christ on Holy Thursday and Good

---

[7]   Fulton J. Sheen, *Those Mysterious Priests* (Garden City, NY: Doubleday, 1974), 30.

Friday, the same mystery re-enacted by every priest, *in persona Christi*, in every Mass he offers. The idea was well-developed by the late John Cardinal O'Connor in a pastoral letter he wrote to his priests in the Archdiocese of New York, *Always a Priest, Always Present*:

> The life of the priest is an extension of the Mass. I believe firmly that powerful as was His preaching, forceful as was His teaching, spectacular as were His miracles, Christ did not make possible the salvation of the world until He suffered and died on the cross. When He appeared utterly helpless, He was most powerful. It is understandable in purely human terms that those who spit in His face and jeered at Him demanded, "If you are the Son of God, prove it by coming down from the cross" (Mt 27:40). Had He come down, He would not have saved the world. He would have been an utter failure. From these reflections, I derive a number of postulates for my own life as a priest. First, I see the Mass as a mysterious spiritual perpetuation of the crucifixion through all of time and space, with a tremendous impact on billions of people, those here present in the world, those long gone, those yet to be born. And from this perspective I view all my activities as a priest as empowered by the Mass in a special way. What do I mean? I see the preaching, teaching and miracles of Christ as empowered to have immediate impact because He was the Son of God. These activities and salvific power, however, only "proactively" reaching forth, as it were, to the crucifixion and deriving their saving power from the suffering and death Christ would undergo. The saving power of the Mass derives from the crucifixion already completed. The activities of the priest, in turn, his preaching and teaching, his dispensing of the sacraments, his various ministries and administrative pursuits—all these derive their salvific power retroac-

tively from the crucifixion. I see all this power as perpetuated through the Mass. For me, then, everything I do during the course of the day is an extension of the Mass, the Mass radiates through every thought, word and action, and fills it with the power of the crucifixion. When I baptize, the sacrament is effective because of the death of Christ, as when I anoint or absolve. When I visit a sickbed, give a premarital instruction, teach a class, the Mass is at work, extending the crucifixion, the death, the resurrection of Christ. This, to me, is a very special way of being "always a priest."[8]

Such, according to Cardinal O'Connor, is the essence of the priesthood. It is first and foremost Christ's priesthood, in which chosen men share, a priesthood described by Henry Edward Cardinal Manning of Westminster, England in the nineteenth century as the office Christ assumed for the redemption of the world by the sacrifice of Himself in the "vestment" of our manhood. Cardinal Manning was very clear what each ordained man shares in:

There are not two priesthoods, as there are not two sacrifices for sin. But one sacrifice has forever redeemed the world, and is offered continually in heaven and on earth; in heaven by the only Priest, before the Eternal Altar; on earth by the multitude and succession of priests who are one with Him as partakers of His priesthood; not as representatives only, but in reality; as also the sacrifice they offer is not a representation only, but His true, real and substantial Body and Blood offered by their hands....[9]

---

8 John J. O'Connor, *Always a Priest, Always Present* (New York: Archdiocese of New York, 1989), 6-7.
9 Henry Edward Manning, *The Eternal Priesthood* (London: Burns and Oates, Ltd., undated), 4.

A curial Cardinal in Rome, speaking to American seminarians some years ago, said he perceived a certain confusion among contemporary students for the ordained priesthood regarding the nature and function of the priestly office. In telling the students there would be no confusion if they but consulted the tradition of the Church, his words took on a prophetic cast. No identity could be clearer, no vocation more unambiguous.

2

The Priesthood of Jesus Christ

Every priest finds the reason for his priestly existence in the priesthood of Jesus Christ, the Eternal High Priest. Some years ago, Jesuit Father Albert Vanhoye, in his study on the Letter to the Hebrews, noted:

> It is through all the realities of our life and death that we go forward to God, by uniting ourselves with the life and death of Christ. Such is the practice of the fundamental Christian priesthood, that which is common to the entire people of God. The place and role of the ministering priesthood entrusted to the clergy of the Church must be understood in this light. The priesthood is sacramental. It constitutes the visible, mediating intervention of Christ in the lives of Christians. Without the ministry of bishops and priests, the union between the life of the Christian and Christ's life could not be objectively brought about… the priestly ministry is indispensable. It is through it that Christ shows objectively His presence and action in the Church and unites believers to His sacrifice.[1]

To the Jewish people, priesthood, or the offering of Temple sacrifice, was limited to individuals of a higher social class whose forebearers had held the same office. John the Baptist,

---

[1] Albert Vanhoye, S.J., *Our Priest is Christ* (Rome: Pontifical Biblical Institute, 1977), 43.

Our Lord's precursor, is a case in point. His father, Zechariah, was a priest, and his mother, Elizabeth, was a descendant of Aaron. In the course of Christ's public life, He never referred to Himself as a priest (only the Letter to the Hebrews makes such a reference). Further, Saint Joseph, His foster father, did not come from the hereditary priestly tribe of Levi; quite the opposite: he was of the house of Judah. Our Blessed Mother's ancestry is shrouded in mystery, which gives rise to the thought that she did not come from a high social standing, but from a more moderate lineage. From these two points, theologians have postulated that the priesthood Christ came to establish would be entirely new: not based on one's family background, and not associated with heredity.

Not only did Christ disclaim the title of priest, He never used any of the descriptives which came to be associated with Him in Christian spirituality. It is as though He and His mission defied linguistic analysis: from the point of discipleship, this only made human hearts burn with more intensified love. For His enemies, however, it was a source of rivalry and suspicion. Members of the Jewish priestly caste came to view Our Lord as a challenge to their authority and position.

Their discussions centered around Temple worship. Christ's telling them "Here... is something greater than the Temple"[2] totally eluded their grasp. The temple of His body contained God in a way human beings could not begin to comprehend, and in making reference to it, He was not attempting to abolish the cultic priesthood as it was; rather, He was trying to raise it to a higher level. When He chased the money changers from the Temple, He was doing something a Jewish priest would be less likely to even attempt; He was laying claim to a higher authority, His heavenly Father.

Scripture scholars have viewed Christ's exchange with Caiaphas, the high priest, as the pinnacle in His dialogue with the Jewish priesthood, and they have carefully studied His

---

[2] Matthew 12:6.

words. During His trial, His accusers raised His earlier asser-
tion "Destroy this temple and I shall raise it up in three days."[3]
Even the Gospel writers note He was speaking of the temple of
His body, and that body was so animated with the life of the
Spirit, His words must imply an entirely new emphasis: He
would inaugurate His eternal priesthood, in which men would
be invited to share. Further into the trial, Our Lord tells
Caiaphas: "From this time onward, you will see the Son of Man
seated at the right hand of the Power and coming on the clouds
of heaven.…" Scholars tell us that in addition to Daniel 7:13, He
was alluding to an ancient prophecy in the Psalms:

> The Lord has sworn and will not change His purpose:
> "You are a priest forever in the succession of Mel-
> chisedech." The Lord at your right hand has broken
> Kings in the day of His anger.[4]

He was, therefore, laying claim to an eternal priesthood, like that
of Melchisedech, not to the Levitical one known to the Jews.
Also, by His use of the term, "from this time onward,"[5] we are
told Our Lord refers to the actual exercise of the priestly office,
the sending of the Holy Spirit upon the Church at Pentecost. In
that gift, the Church came to realize His messiahship had been
fulfilled:

> Exalted thus at God's right hand, He received the Holy
> Spirit from the Father, as was promised, and all that
> you now see and hear flows from Him. For it was not
> David who went up to heaven; his own words are:
> "The Lord said to my Lord, 'Sit at my right hand until
> I make your enemies your footstool'." Let all Israel then
> accept as certain that God has made this Jesus, whom
> you crucified, both Lord and Messiah.[6]

---

[3] John 2:19.
[4] Psalm 110:4.
[5] Matthew 26:64.
[6] Acts 2:34-36.

With Our Lord's priesthood confirmed, it is essential to look more closely at the eternal High Priest Himself. The holiness of Christ came at the moment of His conception, the moment when His mother Mary agreed to give God a human nature:

> In order to enter more deeply into the mystery of this marvelous priestly consecration, let us consider the coming of the angel to Nazareth. Mary is in prayer; she is full of grace. The angel, who has been sent as an ambassador, delivers a message to her. What is the message? That the Word has chosen her womb as the nuptial chamber in which to espouse humanity: "The Holy Spirit will descend upon you," and Mary replies: "Be it done unto me according to thy word" (Luke 1:33-38). At this sacred moment the first priest is consecrated and the voice of the Father resounds in heaven: "Thou art a priest forever according to the order of Melchisedech" (Ps. Cix.4).[7]

Our Lord's consecration unfolds throughout His public life. Like all Jewish children, He was presented in the Temple. In all other cases, the offering of the child's life to God symbolized its need of redemption. With the Divine Child, however, it was no symbolic offering; rather, it was actualized in Mary's acceptance of the sorrow prophesied by the old man, Simeon. Christ's consecration was intensified at His Baptism with the theophany of the Father's delight and the gift of their Spirit. The Son referred to His own consecration, both in the synagogue of Nazareth, where He applied Isaiah's prophecy to Himself (Luke 4:16-21), and when He prayed His priestly prayer of consecration for Himself and all the priests who would be configured to Him (John 17:1-26). The paschal mystery was the culmination of His consecration, a fact which Saint Paul clearly mentioned

---

[7] Dom Columba Marmion, O.S.B., *Christ—The Ideal of the Priest* (London: Sands & Co., Ltd., 1952), 20. Ps. Cix.4 (109:4)=Psalm 110:4. The Greek and Latin versions of the Psalms divided the Psalms a bit differently than the Hebrew version; as a result, the numbering of some Psalms varies slightly.

when he preached that the resurrection had proven Christ Son of God in all His power (Romans 1:4).

His consecration is, therefore, well established as a priest—but not as a priest alone. Our Lord is also a victim, and the two were never meant to be separated:

As the Son of Man He plainly thought that He was the second Adam sent to destroy the work of Satan. It revealed His representational relation, not just to the Jews but to the human race. He was humanity. Pre-eminently, it was the sin-bearing character of His priesthood that came to the fore as He taught: "The Son of Man has nowhere to lay His head" (Matthew 8:20). As a priest, He came among the elect and the people of God; but as a victim, His love reached out "to seek and save what is lost" (Luke 19:10). The sin-bearing character of Christ did not begin on the cross. He was not first a priest and then, during the last three days, a Victim. His Victimhood was never at any one moment divorced from His Priesthood. Pursuit, misjudgment, hunger, thirst, weariness, homelessness, the appearance of greater age (John 8:57) were due to another cause than nature and history alone. The very soul-trouble He felt when the Greeks approached Him, proved how His soul foresaw that death was the condition of victory over sin (John 12:21-27). As the priest, He was *personally* without sin; as the victim, He was *representationally* "made sin."[8]

Our Lord as priest and victim surely had interior dispositions and attitudes which are themselves topics for profound meditation. They were well-captured decades ago by Blessed Columba Marmion, a Dublin-born diocesan priest who entered the Benedictine order in Belgium some seven years after his ordination for his native Archdiocese. He went on to become Prior

---

[8]   Fulton J. Sheen, *Those Mysterious Priests* (Garden City, NY: Doubleday, 1974), 36-37.

of Mont Cesar, Louvain, and later Abbot of Maredsous. Beatified by Pope John Paul II, Marmion became very well known as a spiritual writer and retreat master and was, for several years, the spiritual director of Cardinal Mercier of Malines, Belgium. Generations of priests were nurtured on his writings, and his insights into the mind of Christ are particularly penetrating:

> Let us meditate for a few moments on the mystery of the interior dispositions of Jesus as priest and victim. The attitude of Christ, the Sovereign Priest, was essentially one of profound reverence and adoration. And what was the source of this attitude? The vision of His Father *Patrem immensae Maiestatis.* He knew Him as no other creature can ever know Him: "Just Father, the world hath not known Thee; but I have known Thee" (John xvii, 25). The full depth of the divine perfections were open to His sight: the absolute sanctity of the Father, His sovereign justice, His infinite goodness. This sight filled Him with that reverential fear and that spirit of religion which must animate the offerer of a sacrifice. What was the fundamental attitude of Jesus the Victim? It was likewise adoration, but here it finds expression in the acceptance of destruction and death.
>
> Jesus knew that He was destined to the cross for the remission of the sins of the world; before the divine justice He felt Himself burdened with the crushing weight of all the sins of the world. He gave His full consent to this role of victim. He had not, however, contrition like a penitent who mourns for his own personal faults. But on many occasions He experienced a sadness unto death at seeing Himself overwhelmed by the burden of so much iniquity. Did He not say in the Garden of Olives: "My soul is sorrowful even unto death"? We can see that the attitude of the victim is in perfect conformity with that of the priest.[9]

---

[9] Marmion, *op. cit.*, 21.

Jesus Christ, priest and victim, comes into the world uttering what one author has termed His "Ecce venio" or "Behold, I come." He understood that His dual role was His heavenly Father's eternal plan. The divine Son was the only one ever sent into the world to die; for all others, death is an interruption. For Christ, it was the summit of His earthly life. The shadow of the cross was before Him in all His earthly activities, and His acceptance of that end explains all the other particulars: the human body He assumed from Mary, one which was as capable of fatigue, or suffering or any of the realities human beings know only so well.

Perhaps most significant for all who bear the priestly configuration to Christ is His assuming the role of the Good Shepherd who lays down His life for His sheep. This is intimately linked with Calvary, the death of the God-man, an act so unique, so novel, so unparalleled in human history, that its very unselfishness proves it to be the utmost in sacrifice, the most convincing act of love humanity could ever know. It had been prophesied in Isaiah to be just what it was, not an exercise in personal power, but proof positive of His love for us.

As a shepherd, Christ exercises prophetic, priestly and royal functions. As a prophet, the shepherd teaches His flock— the good news, the Gospel, the message His heavenly Father sent Him into the world to give:

> When, at the beginning of His public life, Jesus describes His own mission, He mentions first the proclamation of the Good News: "The spirit of the Lord has been given to me, for He has anointed me, He has sent me to bring the Good News to the poor, to proclaim liberty to captives and to the blind new sight, to set the downtrodden free, to proclaim the Lord's year of favor" (Luke 4:18-19).[10]

---

[10] Jean Galot, S.J., *Theology of the Priesthood* (San Francisco: Ignatius Press, 1985), 45.

Since he was God-man, He could offer the one perfect sacrifice which did not abolish the ritual sacrifices of the Old Testament, but brought them to perfection. The new Passover, a drama of two parts, sacramental and sacrificial, was to be re-enacted ritually until the end of time. Our Lord saw to it these events would not be left to chance human recollection; rather, they would be brought to life in much the same way the Jews believed their annual memorializing of the Passover brought God's saving actions to the present: this, however, was different; Christ told His followers He wanted them to have the full-ness of life, and if they did not eat His flesh and drink His blood, that life would not be theirs:

> The giving of thanks was admittedly a part of the ritual of the Passover, but may we not legitimately believe that Jesus, at this solemn moment, thanked His Father, not only for His past bounties toward the chosen people, but also for all those of the New Testament. He saw the innumerable multitude of Christians who would refresh themselves at the holy table, who would feed on His adorable flesh and drink of His precious blood. He thanked the Father for all the help which He had destined for His members and especially for His priests until the end of time. Let us not forget that the bosom of the Father is the source from which flows, through Jesus, all mercies and all gifts.[11]

He plainly attested that His kingship transcended this world. His words proved Him, in the minds of His opponents, an en-emy of the state. That kingship, however, was proclaimed by the sign affixed to His cross, and brought to fruition only through His sacrificial death:

> All the supernatural help granted to men springs from the supreme sacertodal immolation of Golgotha. All

---

[11] Marmion, *op. cit.*, 25.

the goodness of God toward us, all the depths of His mercy for us are His replies to the unceasing invocation of the merits of Christ. If the whole human race raised to heaven its cries of distress, it would all be of no avail without Jesus: it is the cry of the Son of God which alone gives value to our supplication. But the drama of Calvary is perpetuated in the bosom of the Church. At the consecration, under the veil of the sacrament, the cry of the blood of Jesus sounds forth anew, for at that moment, all the love, all the obedience, all the suffering of His oblation on the cross are presented to the Father.[12]

There is one remaining aspect of the eternal high priesthood of Jesus Christ which the Letter to the Hebrews beautifully describes:

So now, my friends, the blood of Jesus makes us free to enter boldly into the sanctuary by the new living way which He has opened for us through the curtain, the way of His flesh. We have, moreover, a great priest set over the household of God, so let us make our approach in sincerity of heart and full assurance of faith, our guilty hearts sprinkled clean, our bodies washed with pure water. Let us be firm and unswerving in the confession of our hope, for the Giver of the promise may be trusted. We ought to see how each of us may best arouse others to love and active goodness, not staying away from our meetings, as some do, but rather encouraging one another, all the more because you see the day drawing near.[13]

This is how our closeness with God becomes a reality. A path is open to us, made possible by the shedding of the blood of Christ. Through it, our Lord entered into the new sanctuary

---

[12] *Ibid.*, 28.
[13] Hebrews 10:19-25.

which, we read, was not made with human hands. Therefore, we need never fear death; our individual death united to the death of Christ is our path to eternal life. Christ entered into a tremendous solidarity with humanity through His incarnation, and because of it, our human nature will be able to pass where His already has. Our earthly life completed, we have the promise of sharing fully in the Father's glory, but, through Christ and with Him, we have already begun, ever so mysteriously, to share that life:

> When we celebrate the Holy Sacrifice, we must believe that we enter into this magnificent torrent of praise, that we participate in this liturgy of heaven. Let us realize at the moment when we receive the Blessed Sacrament that for us, as for the blessed, it is the sacred humanity of Jesus alone which puts us in contact with the divinity. As we await the vision and the full clarity of the city of God let it be our joy to repeat: O Jesus, for your elect you are everything! For us also be everything while we march on in the spirit of faith towards the eternal Jerusalem.[14]

---

[14] Marmion, *op. cit.*, 31.

3

Priesthood in the Mind of Saint Paul and Developed in the Early Church

Few there are who would be unfamiliar with the conversion of Saul of Tarsus in 35 A.D. A Jew of the Pharisee party, strongly intent on persecuting Christians, he was thrown from his horse on the Damascus road and asked the question, "Why are you persecuting me?" Not why are you persecuting my Church, but me. We have the beginnings of the doctrine of the Mystical Body of Christ in that statement; we have also the beginnings of the greatest missionary career in the Church. The impressive Basilica of Saint Paul Outside the Walls in the Eternal City is testimony to the apostle who, as a young man, had received a splendid Greek and Jewish education, and who used that education to ultimately preach Christ and Him crucified to the Gentiles. Over two decades, he undertook three great missionary journeys: through Syria and Asia Minor, in Corinth, and around Ephesus in modern Turkey. Initially, he had spent his early Christian years near Damascus, and in 48 A.D., at the height of his career, he was part of a delegation sent from Antioch to Jerusalem to discuss the status of Gentile believers in the early Church. Jerusalem would also be the scene of his arrest, caught up as he was in the earliest persecutions of the Church. Paul's Roman citizenship enabled him to have final recourse in the capital of the Empire, but house arrest was all that awaited him. He was martyred in Rome sometime between 62 and 67 A.D.

During his third missionary journey (53-57 A.D.), he wrote the letters which form such an integral part of the New Testament. In none of them does he specifically describe Christ as a priest, nor does he outline a unique theology of the priesthood. Rather, he concentrates on the sacrificial death of the God-man, Jesus Christ, as being the one perfect sacrifice which transcends all the sacrifices of the Old Covenant. Also, he specifically uses the term "ministry" to describe his apostolate. The word has taken on an overuse in the twenty-first century, but Paul was quite specific that its meaning comprised three functions: preaching, governing, and the offering of sacrifice. Preaching meant evangelizing, which in turn meant bringing the forgiveness of Christ to believers, a forgiveness which remitted sin and put sinners on the road to salvation. Paul also related preaching, or evangelizing, to leadership, especially over those churches where he exercised a paternal servant role. Finally, he writes that he received a command to offer the chalice of the New Covenant as a memorial of Christ. All of these he viewed as his "ministry."

Pauline scholars refer to the apostle's threefold vocation: a minister of the New Covenant, a steward of God's mysteries, and a co-worker with God. The word *covenant*, for Jews, always meant the very personal relationship God made with His chosen people. In his Second Letter to the Corinthians, Paul is very clear that the object of his evangelization is an entirely new covenant, one which is given "... not in a written document, but in a spiritual bond; for the written law condemns to death, but the Spirit gives life" (3:6). Herein lies a fundamental difference between the Jewish and Christian priesthoods; the former ministered only to the maintenance of the law, while the latter, animated by the Spirit, touched one's person at the very core of his being, bringing God to man, and making man holy:

> The ministry seeks to let "radiate the light of the knowledge of God's glory, the glory on the face of Christ" (2 Corinthians 4:6). God's true face becomes revealed in

Christ. In the Old Covenant, God's face remained concealed by a veil. Only Christ removes that veil. Hence, the ministry of the New Covenant makes it possible to contemplate the Lord openly, so that those who do so may be transformed in his image (2 Corinthians 3:14-18). The purpose of the ministry is, then, to let God be seen.[1]

God is seen in two ways; the work of evangelization enables a person to remove the obstacles in his path to God, allowing him to see more clearly and appreciate more fully the God who loves him so much. Sanctification, as Paul develops it in his Second Letter to the Corinthians, lies in the fact that God has "reconciled us men to Himself through Christ, and He has enlisted us in this service of reconciliation" (5:18). One who is called to sanctity is called, not to chastise people for their sins as did the Old Testament prophets, but to preach the salvific death of Christ, the perfect sacrifice offered once for the world's redemption.

Those who offer the Eucharistic sacrifice, so identifiable in the Catholic mind as "ministers of the New Covenant" find their role confirmed in Saint Paul's First Letter to the Corinthians. Our Lord's command to perpetuate His sacrifice throughout all time finds stronger expression here than in the Synoptic Gospels:

> For the tradition which I handed on to you came to me from the Lord Himself: that the Lord Jesus, on the night of His arrest, took bread and, after giving thanks to God, broke it and said: "This is my body which is for you; do this as a memorial of me." In the same way, He took the cup after supper, and said: "This cup is the new covenant sealed by my blood. Whenever you drink it do this as a memorial of me." Every time you eat this bread and drink this cup, you proclaim the death of the Lord, until He comes.[2]

---

[1] Jean Galot, S.J., *Theology of the Priesthood* (San Francisco: Ignatius Press, 1985), 97.
[2] 1 Corinthians 11:23-25.

Paul makes it known that he is not only a minister of the New Covenant, but also a steward of God's mysteries:

> A steward is a person who takes the place of another, who acts in another's name. Paul proclaims himself the servant of Christ and rejects anything that might look like a claim to acting in his own name, any striving after personal renown. He adds, "What is expected of stewards is that each one should be found worthy of his trust" (1 Corinthians 4:2). He recalls that he will have to give an account of his own fidelity to Christ and stress his total dependence on him. Stewardship also implies authority, the power to administer "the mysteries of God." In the eyes of Paul, the term "mystery" refers to the plan of salvation which, "kept secret for endless ages," is "now so clear that it must be broadcast to pagans everywhere" through the apostolic proclamation (Romans 16:25-26). To proclaim Christ means to disclose this mystery and, in the act of disclosing it, to fulfill it.[3]

Hence the idea of both preaching and authority are to be found in the stewardship theme. Saint Paul as a preacher has always had enormous consequences for priests. Pope Saint Pius X saw this very clearly in the early years of the twentieth century, and spoke to it in his repeated instructions on preaching to priests throughout the world. Pius' successor, Benedict XV, went even further and issued an encyclical letter on the subject of preaching the word of God: *Humani Generis*. The year was 1917 and the background was a war-torn Europe, a world anxious to hear that divine word. The Holy Father concentrated on Saint Paul as a preacher, and his significance for preachers of all times. Benedict saw three interior dispositions coming to every priest-preacher who made Saint Paul his own: indifference to self, acceptance of suffering, and a spirit of prayer. The

---

[3] Galot, *op. cit.*, 99.

first, indifference to self, meant seeing the will of God for us and doing it:

> No sooner had he been touched by the power of the Lord Jesus, while on his way to Damascus, than he uttered that cry worthy of Saint Paul: "Lord, what wilt thou have me do?" From that moment, and ever afterwards, toil and rest, want and abundance, praise and contempt, even life and death, all alike were for Christ. There can be no doubt that the reason for the extraordinary success of his apostolate was that he completely submitted himself to the will of God. Every preacher, therefore, who strives for the salvation of souls must likewise give first place to this submission to God's will, he should not be concerned to know who are the audience, or what success or what fruits his words will bring; let him think only of God and not of himself.[4]

Acceptance of suffering meant not shrinking from any form of toil or tribulation, much as the Apostle to the Gentiles had done, to the point of confinement in prison and martyrdom:

> If a preacher excels in patient endurance of toil, this washes away his own human failings and wins for him the grace of God so that his toil may be fruitful; moreover, it is astonishing to see how it serves to commend his labours to the Christian people.[5]

Finally, a spirit of prayer, humble prayer before God as the Acts of the Apostles related of Paul:

> In the third place we learn from the apostle that the spirit of prayer is necessary for the preacher; as soon as he was called to the apostolate, he began to pray

---

[4] Benedict XV, *Humani Generis*, cited in *The Catholic Priesthood: According to the Teaching of the Church* (Dublin: M.H. Gill and Son, Ltd., 1957), 114. This encyclical of Benedict XV is not to be confused with the later encyclical of the same title issued by Pius XII.

[5] *Ibid.*, 115.

humbly to God: "For behold he prayeth." It is not by a flow of words, or by subtle discussions or by vehement perorations, that the salvation of souls is accomplished; the preacher who goes no further is only a "sounding brass or a tinkling symbol." It is divine grace that gives vigour and wonderful power to the words of men: "God gave the increase."[6]

"I am like a skilled master builder," Saint Paul wrote, "who by God's grace laid the foundation, and someone else is putting up the building."[7] The Corinthians, to whom he wrote, were themselves God's building. Paul was merely the beginner builder, God's co-worker, who began the initial enterprising of building this new Temple. The structure itself was to be built up in the Lord, and corresponds to the Church. This structure, made possible by the resurrection of Christ, is fitted into a living Temple through the power of the Spirit dwelling in all of the members and transforming them.

Saint Paul not only bequeathed his own legacy to our understanding of the priesthood, but in his Letter to the Colossians, began the Church's understanding of apostolic ministry in the New Testament:

> First and foremost, I handed on to you the facts which had been imparted to me: that Christ died for our sins, in accordance with the Scriptures; that He was buried; that He was raised to life on the third day, according to the Scriptures; and that he appeared to Cephas, and afterwards to the Twelve.[8]

Few scriptural passages, if any, take us further into the origin of the Christian religion. Paul is giving an oral tradition about accredited witnesses to the resurrection, one which schol-

---

[6] *Ibid.*
[7] 1 Corinthians 3:10.
[8] Colossians 15:3-5.

ars assume he received while he himself was a catechumen, no more than five years after the death of Christ.

As the Church developed, the Synoptic Gospels provide us even more information into the beginnings of the apostolic ministry. Each of the three writers concentrate on the vocation of the Twelve, with Mark specifically referring to their initiation into the "mystery of the Kingdom" (4:11). They received a specific authority stemming from their intimacy with Christ, and their complete familiarity with His gospel:

> Matthew, Mark and Luke describe this authority in three ways. First of all, Jesus entrusts to the Twelve the worship or cultus of the New Covenant. They receive the command to baptize, issued in the great Commission at the end of Matthew. And, above all, they are made the vehicles of the tradition about the institution of the Eucharist, and receive the command to celebrate it in remembrance of Jesus—for his anamnesis, something stronger in biblical Greek, with its Old Testament background, than our word "remembrance." For the Eucharist is the cultic act whereby, in transforming the Church's gifts of bread and wine, the Holy Spirit brings the person of Christ and the power of His saving sacrifice into our present. Secondly, the Twelve are given a unique teaching role. They become the accredited recipients of its message, the "kerygma," and the representatives of the teaching Christ, so that anyone who hears the Twelve hears Jesus Himself, and thereby the Father who sent Him.... Lastly, in the Synoptic presentation, the authority of the Twelve is also a matter of power or government. The Twelve are plenipotentiaries who will rule the new Israel, the community of the Kingdom (Matthew 19:28; Luke 22:28-30). Although their power is to be exercised in humility, in a spirit of service, it is a genuine governing authority, ordered to the unity of God's people and its faithfulness to His plan.[9]

---

[9]   Aidan Nichols, O.P., *Holy Order* (Dublin: Veritas, 1990), 6-8.

These three tasks correspond to the priestly, prophetic and kingly offices of Christ; as a priest, He dispenses the Father's grace (which is essentially the work of the Holy Spirit in souls); as a prophet, He instructs us about the Father, and the Father's specific plan for our final end; and as a king, He will hand over His Kingdom to the Father at the consummation of the world.

Saint John the Evangelist is in fundamental accord with the Synoptic writers, viewing the ministry of the Twelve as priestly, prophetic and kingly:

> Through the Twelve, the Son will communicate to the whole Church, not only life everlasting, the grace of the Kingdom, but also the knowledge of the Father and the Son: a knowledge, bound up with the prophetic office, which is both a doctrinal grasp of what the Father and the Son have done for our salvation and a mysteric, sympathetic understanding of their relation to each other and to ourselves, and so a communion with them. Finally, and related this time to the pastoral or kingly office, the Twelve are to render the community of Jesus a unity—and not just any kind of unity but one which reflects the unbreakable unity of Father and Son themselves.[10]

The Twelve, of course, correspond to today's bishops, in that bishops are the successors of the apostles. A question arises about the origin of those who assist the bishops: priests and deacons. In the Acts of the Apostles we find a description of the ordination of the Seven, the first such event to be recounted in the life of the Church.[11] It is the reading traditionally proclaimed at Diaconate ordinations and felt by many to be the formal institution of the Diaconate. Another school of thought, however, dating from Saint John Chrysostom, is dubious. Scholars note that a dispute arose over the Greek terms *diakonia* and *diakonein*.

---

[10] *Ibid.*, 11.
[11] Acts 6:2-6.

They have the meaning of service, and particularly the distribution of food, but such distribution could well have been done in the city of Jerusalem by fewer than seven men. A religious interpretation of the text (as opposed to a social one), seems to suggest itself, with the calling of the whole Christian community to be present, the fact that men "filled with the Holy Spirit and wisdom" were sought, and, when selected, the imposition of hands was performed over them. At least one theologian has suggested this account in Acts must be coupled with yet other descriptions which speak of the early Christians meeting "constantly to hear the Apostles teach, and to share the common life, and to pray,"[12] noting that those same Apostles "went steadily on with their preaching in the Temple, and in private houses, telling the Good News of Jesus the Messiah."[13] Such passages give even further support to the view that the service of the Seven transcended the social order:

> The Seven do not act as delegates of the community. The rite of institution performed by the Apostles comprises a prayer followed by the imposition of hands. The public prayer implores the action of the Holy Spirit, and the imposition of hands implies the imparting of sacred powers, which is the import of this gesture in Jewish tradition (cf. Numbers 27:18f; Deuteronomy 34:9). How then are we to describe the Seven? Luke abstains from giving them a title, which means that no title was bestowed on them at the moment of institution. The institution was new and had no name. The account indicates that the Seven were empowered by the Apostles to preside at the service of the tables, that is, at the meal with which the Eucharist was brought to a close. This empowerment extended to the proclamation of the Good News, a proclamation which, as Luke explicitly notes, took place

---

[12] Acts 2:42.
[13] Acts 5:42.

"daily" both in private homes and in the Temple.... It
seems, then, that the ordination of the Seven should be
regarded as a "presbyterial" ordination.
But we should bear in mind that at the beginning,
the term "presbyter" is used without precision. True,
the Seven are not named presbyters. It may well be that
this title was not suitable for them, since they belonged
to the Hellenistic community. Certain indications lead
us to believe that they were later assigned to the same
rank, more or less, as the presbyters.[14]

The Seven were not called presbyters, though research
indicates there were very likely presbyters in Jerusalem before
the ordination of the Seven. Individuals referred to as "the Hebrews" were thought to be presbyters, those who were at the
service of the Apostles. They are mentioned as being present at
the Council of Jerusalem, the earliest council of the Church, and
that presence would indicate their existence from the very out-
set of the Church's life. Their origin is very likely in the original seventy-two disciples, and that presence among the seventy-
two, along with their closeness to Christ, would guarantee the
permanence and particulars of their life's work, and the gift of
the Holy Spirit at Pentecost served as their priestly ordination.
The Acts of the Apostles refers to "brothers," and by the
time of the Council of Jerusalem, "elders." Both were likely early
titles, and the term "presbyter," it is claimed, became normative after the ordination of the Seven, to claim their seniority
over those so recently ordained. As the Church spread geo-
graphically, presbyters were appointed to the new Christian
communities, and with the passage of time, their role became
clearly defined, their position the subject of meditation by the
early Church Fathers.

---

[14] Galot, *op. cit.*, 162-163.

4

Priestly Developments in the Patristic Age

Basil the Great and Gregory Nazianzen often referred to the Council Fathers at Nicea in 325 A.D. as the "Fathers of the Church." The term endured, and came to include a much larger group of individuals whose writings, taken collectively, defended the faith of the Church. They were among the earliest of apologists, and are to be found both prior to, and following, the Council of Nicea. For this reason, scholars are wont to divide their writings into pre- and post-Nicene periods. One studies their work to discover the contents of orthodoxy in the early Church, and also to trace the development of doctrine. These Fathers contributed significantly to the Church's understanding of Holy Orders: the episcopacy, the priesthood, the diaconate.

The pre-Nicene period has its origins in the mid to late second century, and writing centers on the office and functions of bishops. Saint Irenaeus of Lyon, in his work *Against the Heresies*, noted that the entire Christian community should pay careful heed to those "presbyters" who have their succession from the Apostles. Such ones, Irenaeus said, have received the "infallible charism of truth." It is curious he referred to them as presbyters, since this term would eventually be applied only to priests. Clarity in terminology had not yet been achieved, but once the apostolic age ended with the death of the last Apostle,

John the Evangelist, it was clear that there were successors to the Lord's closest collaborators:

> Their office, status, power was unique. No one ever put in a claim to be an Apostle of the second generation. Because of the fact which constituted them Apostles, they were necessarily irreplaceable. To their authority succeeded the new hierarchy of episcopoi and presbyteroi, and as it took their place, this new hierarchy itself underwent a change. The college of episcopoi or presbyteroi who, under the Apostles, had ruled the local church, gave place to an arrangement where in each local church there was but one episcopus whom a number of subordinates, now termed presbyteroi, assisted.[1]

The tendency in each of the local Christian communities to have one bishop developed early on. One reason was practical; one leader would have a much easier time ruling and making decisions, hence when a strong leader emerged, he easily moved into the role of bishop. Also, when heresies began to emerge in the middle of the second century, an emphasis began to be placed on one central figure of authority who could reinforce Catholic teaching. Finally, a theological reason was present: Christ was one divine person, the God-man, and was seen as the model for communal authority.

The question of how bishops became successors of the Apostles (since in earliest times some communities had leaders who had not specifically received authority from the Apostles), find some of its answer in a letter Clement of Rome wrote to the Corinthians, in which he speaks of "eminent persons" to describe men specifically sent by the Apostles to guide local communities. Two theories have been advanced to explain apostolic succession: either those "eminent persons" became lo-

---

[1] Philip Hughes, *A History of the Church* (London: Sheed and Ward, 1934), I, 50.

cal bishops, or they came into the Christian communities and conferred such authority on a man considered a natural leader, through the imposition of hands, doing the same in one locale after another.

When Irenaeus wrote of the Apostles' successors possessing the "infallible charism of truth," he was writing against the background of the Gnostic and Montanist heresies. The former held that salvation is by knowledge, the possession of only a few, while the latter emphasized the direct inspiration of the Holy Spirit in people's lives, distinct from the teaching Church. With such threats to faith, Irenaeus felt compelled to draw up a list of the apostolic succession, tracing the lineage of each bishop back to an Apostle. This demonstrated that the bishops were the only form of authority concerning doctrine since they were in line with the Apostles, and ultimately with Christ Himself. In addition, the Roman Christian writer, Tertullian, argued that the existence of the different Christian communities were themselves proof of an apostolic succession.

Just as Christ was priest, prophet and king, the bishop, possessing the fullness of the priesthood, shares in these three offices. His kingly, or pastoral role was emphasized by Irenaeus to defend the faith. Such was also seen in his prophetic office, as he taught the faithful sound doctrine. There was also an emphasis on his liturgical, or priestly role. The right of presiding at the Eucharistic liturgy was reserved only to bishops, and by the third century, the Christian writer Hippolytus was referring to the bishop as the "high priest." The term had not been previously used for fear its meaning would be confused with a similar title applied to the pagan priesthood. In time, however, its meaning was more properly linked with the Old Testament priesthood in which the high priest occupied a unique and superior position in the community. As Christian "high priest," the bishop baptizes and confirms new Christians, ordains presbyters, and presides over the Eucharist. He was seen as the one who united the local Christian community to himself and each other. He also unites it to all other Christian communities since he himself is united to his brother bishops in the apostolic succession. When Saint Cyprian of Carthage wrote his work, *On the Unity of the Church*, he described this unity of the clergy and laity as a reflection of the unity of the three divine persons in one God.

Cyprian's analogy has become classic, and taken in its components, it underscored the belief that a bishop was the one authority, the one priest, the one preacher, the one leader of a diocese, and the one administrator. This would later come to be symbolized in the bishop's "cathedra," or throne, found in his cathedral church, a symbol of the throne of God, as Moses had envisioned it, and a symbol of the bishop's doctrinal authority, just as Moses was teacher of the Jews.

The designation of bishops was not uniform. In the early Church, Rome had not yet achieved a pre-eminent position among other dioceses, and papal nominations were not formalized until many centuries later. The most common expression of choice was election by the Christian community, though this in no way implies the Church was a democracy. Rather, God was the source of authority transferred to a bishop by the imposition of hands. The community was simply giving testimony to whether a particular individual was worthy:

> Nomination to the office, even by the Apostle, does not of itself suffice. Before the candidate can act, something more is required. There is mention always of fasting, or prayer, and of the imposition of hands, and always this imposition is the act of those already possessed of authority. As a later, more technical language will describe it, the power of Order, like the power of jurisdiction, like the faith itself, is transmitted from one generation to the next through the action of those who already possess it. Nowhere is it spoken of as coming from below as a result of popular holiness, ability, or the possession of charismata. Though the word is not

yet mentioned, the all-important fact is clear that, for the first generation of Christians, no powers were valid, no teaching guaranteed, no authority was lawful save such as came through the Apostles.[2]

In the decades prior to the Council of Nicea, it is clear that the succession the bishops inherited from the Apostles manifested itself in the development of their priestly, prophetic and kingly functions. Depending on which period of time one refers to, or which author one chooses to cite, one of the three offices is stressed. What is less clear, and only discernable by the third century, was the role of presbyters and deacons in the Church, and their relationship to their bishop. Hippolytus, in his *Apostolic Tradition* refers to the presbyter's role as one of governing and teaching. The gradual development of the functions of the presbyter seemed to parallel those of the bishop. As the bishop takes more doctrinal authority in the community, the priest also develops in the same area, but always dependent on the bishop's own authority. The presbyter's functions are delegated by the bishop; when a bishop was unable to be present to celebrate the Eucharist, a presbyter would then celebrate it. Such was also true of preaching. Hippolytus noted that a deacon was ordained only to be of service to the bishop, and not to be a member of the presbyterate. Once the three orders are in place, there is some doubt as to the liturgical role each occupied:

> In the pre-Nicene age, it is sometimes difficult to distinguish the special liturgical functions of the presbyter from those of the bishop above him or, again, from the deacon below.... It is assumed that all three orders are present together, very much a collaborative co-presence. But the general principle would seem to be that the deacon, being only the liturgical assistant to the bishop, cannot act by himself: above all, at the Eu-

---

[2] *Ibid.*, 51.

charist. When, during the great persecution under
Diocletian and his successors at the start of the fourth
century, some deacons took it upon themselves to celebrate the Eucharist in the absence of bishop or presbyter, they were severely rebuked by two western
councils of the Church.[3]

As one gets closer to 325 A.D., and the first major gathering of the Church Fathers, writers begin to trace the bishop's
liturgical and pastoral functions to specific apostolic origins; his
responsibility for orthodoxy and his power to ordain are similarly traceable. As a result, the episcopal and presbyterial offices
assume a lasting distinction:

> ... to the question of the function of the episcopoi and
> presbyteroi, and the relation of the two classes to each
> other, one view is that the presbyteros was a man to
> whom was given a title of honor for special service, a
> distinction which of itself carried with it no power or
> authority. From among the presbyteroi, the
> episcopoi—whose duty it was, under the Apostle, to
> rule, to teach—were naturally elected. Whence the fact
> that not all presbyteroi were also episcopoi. Later, the
> presbyteroi who are not also episcopoi disappear. The
> name, however, survives and is henceforth used for the
> subordinate officials of the new system, successors in
> part of the old episcopoi, but successors with very re-
> stricted powers and with no authority independent of
> the bishop—as we may now call him.[4]

Not only were their roles clear, but foundations were laid
for further development:

> As the early liturgical sources present ordination, the
> sacramental laying on of hands so consecrates the

---

[3] Aidan Nichols, O.P., *Holy Order* (Dublin: Veritas Publications, 1990), 42-43.
[4] Hughes, *op. cit.*, 50-51.

bishop and presbyter that they are, at a level which only the Holy Spirit can reach, suitably transformed. A new bond with the Son and Spirit is forged, so that the candidate is empowered to act by their strength in that ministry to which his ordination deputes him. We have here the seeds of the doctrine of the priestly "character," a doctrine which will play a major part in the theology of Order in centuries to come.[5]

In the period following Nicea, bishops began to exert more authority, especially in Church councils, once a precedent had been clearly set. Presbyters were more frequently referred to as priests; examples from the year 360 A.D. are the memorials to deceased "priests" found in churches throughout Asia Minor. With the rapid growth of the Church in so many parts of the world, priests began to represent their bishops on the parochial level; the concept of the parish priest, as subsequent centuries would refer to him, became prevalent in the late fourth century, and a definite theology of the priesthood began to emerge. The role of the priest as a pastor, and even more as a teacher was taken up by such saintly writers as Ambrose of Milan and Gregory Nazianzen. Any teacher, Ambrose felt, had to be guided by the highest ethical and moral principles, and when he wrote his work, *On the Duties of Ministers*, the steps he suggested to arrive at the spiritual standards he proposed sounded very reminiscent of the steps one would follow to achieve military fitness. Such is not strange, given Ambrose's background as a Roman provincial governor. Gregory, on the other hand, much the way Saint Paul emphasized when he wrote to the Christians at Ephesus, sees priests guiding others to perfection:

> [T]he guiding of man, that most variable and manifold of creatures, seems to me in very deed to be the art of arts and the sciences of sciences. Any one may recog-

---

5 Nichols, *op. cit.*, 47.

nize this by comparing the work of the physicians of souls with the treatment of the body; and noticing that, laborious as the latter is, ours is more laborious, and of more consequence, from the nature of its subject matter, the power of its science, and the object of its exercise.[6]

Saint Augustine of Hippo, who had converted from a life of hedonistic rationalism, and had been baptized by Ambrose in 387 A.D., also contributed significantly to an early understanding of the priesthood. Many heresies had abounded in the early Church, including Donatism, which Augustine had strongly refuted. Over two hundred seventy African bishops had agreed with its tenets, that sacraments administered by unworthy priests (i.e., those living in a state of serious sin) were invalid. A question then arose about the many priests who had capitulated to this, or any other erroneous doctrine. Saint Augustine forcefully maintained that the spiritual indisposition of those administering the sacrament in no way invalidated its efficacy. It was administered validly, though not licitly. If anything was lacking, Augustine felt, it was the full effect of the sacrament; all potential graces might not flow to the recipient if the priest were living sinfully. By the same token, such graces could be received later should the priest repent and be reconciled to God's grace. In time, Augustine's distinction of valid, but illicit became normative.

Saint John Chrysostom, known for his great eloquence, produced his work, *On the Priesthood*, in 388 A.D. A very practical man, he had meditated profoundly before writing and considered the many practical points a priest should weigh about

---

6   St. Gregory Nazianzen, *Oratio* 2, translated as: "In defence of his flight to Pontus, and his return after his ordination to the priesthood, with an exposition of the character of the priestly office," in C.G. Browne and T.E. Swallow (trs.), *Select Orations of S. Gregory Nazianzen—Nicene and Post-Nicene Fathers*, N.S. 10 (Oxford-New York, 1896), pp. 1-90, cited in *Ibid.*, 61.

his life: he must be studied enough to refute heretics, calm enough not to lose control of his emotions with the many temperaments of people he dealt with, temperate enough that his own life not be given to overindulgence. At the same time, Chrysostom stressed the august nature of the priestly office; the sacrifice he offered was the very death of Christ, in no way comparable to the sacrifices of Old Testament priests:

> Though the office of the priesthood is exercised on earth, it ranks nevertheless, in the order of celestial things—and rightly so. It was neither man nor angel nor an archangel nor any other created power, but the Paraclete himself who established this ministry, and who ordained that men abiding in the flesh should imitate the ministry of the angels. For that reason, it behooves the bearer of the priesthood to be as pure as if he stood in the very heavens amidst those powers.[7]

Pope Saint Gregory the Great's *Pastoral Rule* is yet another major contribution to patristic priestly literature, combining monastic spirituality with the priest's daily life. The emperor Charlemagne was so impressed with Gregory's thought, he presented a copy of his work to each new bishop consecrated within the empire. It centered on the concepts of simplicity and self-discipline, so essential to priestly fidelity. The biblical Old Testament origins of monasticism stressed the individual and the sort of ascetic purity that was seen in the life of John the Baptist. From the New Testament there was an emphasis on the community of believers in Christ and the study of all that tradition had to offer. A priest should, therefore, not neglect the internal life of his soul while tending to the many external duties his office imposed on him.

Finally, the post-Nicene years saw the beginnings of both

---

[7] St. John Chrysostom, *On the Priesthood* IV, 5, from W.A. Jurgens, tr., *The Priesthood. A translation of the 'Peri Hierosynes' of S. John Chrysostom* (New York, 1955), cited in *Ibid.*, 63-64.

a discipline and spirituality of celibacy, though it would be the eleventh century before such was mandated in the West. The Council of Chalcedon in 451 was the first major, though indirect, endorsement of celibacy, which had existed alongside a married clergy from the earliest beginnings of the Church. While married bishops, presbyters and deacons could be found since the apostolic age, equally strong documentary proof exists attesting to the practice of celibacy as being an ancient and time-honored tradition. Hippolytus wrote of it in a very positive way in the third century, and some two hundred years later, Pope Leo the Great could write to a bishop:

> The law of continence is the same for the ministers of the altar, for the bishops and for the priests; when they were (still) lay people or lectors, they could freely take a wife and beget children. But once they have reached the ranks mentioned above, what had been permitted is no longer so.[8]

When Leo spoke of the "law of continence," he was referring to legislation applying specifically to married clergy, namely abstinence from marital relations. If there was a moral prohibition against bishops, priests and deacons having marital relations once in orders, such commitment would be a major impediment to marriage for those aspiring to priestly vocations. There was a desired uniformity even at this early period of the Church's life, and celibacy received strong endorsement from such writers as Ambrose, Augustine, and Jerome. Specific legislation was seen for the first time at the Council of Elvira, affecting Spanish clergy:

---

[8]   *Epist. Ad Rusticum Narbonensem Episcopum, Inquis*, 111, Resp. PL 54, 1204a, cited in Roman Cholis, "Priestly Celibacy in Patristics and in the History of the Church" in *For Love Alone: Reflections on Priestly Celibacy* (Middlegreen, Slough: ST PAULS, 1993), 33.

> We decree that all bishops, priests and deacons in the
> service of the ministry are entirely forbidden to have
> conjugal relations with their wives and to beget chil-
> dren; should anyone do so, let him be excluded from
> the honor of the clergy.[9]

There was a spiritual basis for this; dedicated continence
was seen as a basis for a life of priestly prayer. Further, a sharp
distinction was made by patristic writers between the Old Testament priesthood, where continence was practiced only peri-
odically when the priests were functioning in the Temple, offering sacrifices, and the New Testament priest, acting as a
mediator between God and man, offering the same sacrifices as
the God-man. The latter priest was not involved in some temporary occupation, but in a total giving of himself for life, what
later generations of writers would come to call a configuration
to Christ.

---

[9]   *Ibid.*, 34.

5

Medieval, Reformation, Counter-Reformation Mind on the Priesthood

Blessed Columba Marmion produced a significant number of spiritual works, among which was a compilation of retreat conferences to priests entitled *Christ—The Ideal of the Priest*. In it, he offers a stirring description of the change occurring in a man who has received Holy Orders:

> Remember what happens on the day of Ordination. On that blessed morning, a young levite, overwhelmed by the sentiment of his own unworthiness and weakness, prostrates himself before the bishop who represents the heavenly Pontiff; he bows his head under the imposition of hands by the consecrating prelate. At this moment the Holy Ghost descends upon him and the eternal Father is able to contemplate with ineffable complacency this new priest, a living reproduction of His beloved Son: *Hic est Filius meus dilectus*. While the bishop holds his hand extended and the whole assembly of priests imitate his gesture, the words of the angel addressed to the Virgin Mary are accomplished anew: "The Holy Ghost shall come upon thee and the power of the Most High shall overshadow thee" (Luke 1:35). At this moment, full of mystery, the Holy Ghost takes possession of this chosen one of the Lord, and effects between Christ and him an eternal resemblance;

when he rises, he is a man transformed: "Thou art a priest forever, according to the order of Melchisedech" (Psalm 109:4 [110:4]).[1]

The "eternal resemblance," or transformation of which Marmion speaks, is another way of describing the "character" of Orders. This character has been studied for generations, and has its origins in the writings of Saint Paul in the New Testament. The apostle speaks of those who have been marked with a seal (2 Corinthians 1:22; Ephesians 1-3, 4:30). The seal is an indelible one, making a lasting imprint on all the baptized, giving them access to salvation, making them heirs of the Kingdom of Heaven. The baptized become sharers in the priesthood of the faithful, hence the sacrament may be received only once in the course of a lifetime.

The priestly seal, or character, is separate from, yet much related to the baptismal one. It, too, may be received only once, imprints something permanent on the soul, and follows naturally from the characters given at Baptism and Confirmation. Saint Augustine was the first to write of the sacramental character of Holy Orders, and he viewed its permanence as completely unaffected by one's leaving the priestly ministry, sinning morally, or in any way separating oneself from Christ's Mystical Body; a priest is always a priest.

The Middle Ages had known a variety of opinions on the nature of the sacramental character of ordination. William of Auvergne, Thomas Aquinas, Duns Scotus, and many other theologians had wrestled with the question and describe it in such terms as: holiness, a capacity to be acted upon, a disposition, a figure, a sign that signifies grace, a habitus, a sign of participation in the sacraments, a sign of the profession of faith, a relation, and a cultic empowerment. The latter was the thought of Aquinas, and came to enjoy enormous prestige in Catholic

---

[1]   Dom Columba Marmion, O.S.B., *Christ—The Ideal of the Priest* (London: Sands & Co., Ltd., 1952), 49.

thought, very much eclipsing the others. Translated into the modern idiom, Thomas might have described it in this fashion:

> The priest is a man of power and authority. By his preaching, example and counsel, he directs the lives of his parishioners in accordance with the revealed wisdom of God and the laws of the Church. In his administration of the sacraments and blessings of the Church, he is the human channel through which the power of the Passion of Christ is transmitted to men for their salvation. No man could give himself such power or arrogate to himself such authority. No mere man could even dare to choose himself for so stupendous a role in the life of men. Only God can make a man a priest, and He does so in the sacrament of Holy Orders.[2]

Thomas stresses the uniqueness of this particular sacrament; unique not in what it does for a recipient, but what it empowers him to do for others:

> When a man becomes a priest, he becomes another Christ. Before his ordination he received a grace from others. But after ordination he can communicate grace to others. He is the active, human instrument through which the grace of Christ passes to men. This makes it apparent that Holy Orders is a social sacrament. Baptism, Confirmation, Communion, Penance and Extreme Unction sanctify the individual for his own advantage. But Holy Orders sanctifies a man for the benefit of others. It makes him holy so that he can communicate holiness to others.[3]

In the sixteenth century, the Council of Trent tried to clarify the meaning of the indelible character, and from its teaching the

---

[2] Walter Farrell, O.P. and Martin J. Healy, S.T.D., *My Way of Life* (Brooklyn: Confraternity of the Precious Blood, 1952), 569.
[3] *Ibid.*, 571.

Church began to speak of an ontological change taking place in each recipient. Beyond that, the Council did not define the character with a precision. Specifically, nothing was said about the nature of the priestly character after death—whether it endures in eternal life. Such has been meditated on, however, in very positive fashion:

> The mark is "indelible." Its permanency is not dependent on whether you or I have what it takes to carry out an activity. Nothing can erase it, nothing can cause it to vanish. The indelibility affirmed by the Council applies at least to this our earthly life during which the sacrament may never be repeated. As to its permanency in the next life, nothing has been explicitly declared. The Council's own declaration was not intended to address this issue, which is rather speculative and without direct relevance in the life of the Church here and now. But since the character is a spiritual mark, it is difficult to see how death could prevail against it.[4]

Theologians readily admit they are dealing with a mystery. One has to begin with the characters of the sacraments of Baptism and Confirmation, and the graces received from them. These sacraments orient the direction of one's life in Christ; when a man chooses Holy Orders, he builds upon an already existing spiritual foundation by receiving yet another indelible seal configuring him to Christ, and changing his very being, so that all his thoughts, attitudes, and actions correspond to the mission of the priesthood. This is a gift from God, totally consuming the existence of the chosen man:

> [W]e can well understand how the value of the priestly character is both ontological and dynamic. It is ontological because the priestly character affects personal

---

[4] Jean Galot, S.J., *Theology of the Priesthood* (San Francisco: Ignatius Press, 1985), 198.

being not more superficially than Baptism—namely, only for the sake of the function to be exercised—but more thoroughly by bringing oneself to bear upon the person's deepest feelings. It seeks to surrender to God, not only deeds, but the very source from which springs the doing of deeds, the human being itself with all its capacities and possibilities.[5]

All of this is seen more clearly in light of the heavenly Father's relation to His divine Son, and the character bestowed on the Son's being. It is one of profound depth, the same depth that characterizes the link between who Christ is and what He does:

> Once the priestly character is again set in this original perspective, it can be understood as the Father's imprint on the Son, an imprint which, at the Incarnation, makes of the man Jesus the image of the supreme Shepherd. This constitutive imprint of Christ's fundamental priesthood goes on to impress itself on each one of those who receive a participation in His pastoral ministry. The Father who "inscribes His own self" on the Son inscribes that same self on priests in a very special way. What Jesus was in His own priesthood, as Word become flesh, namely, the Father's inscription and signature on a human life—an inscription that 'recounts' the ineffable (John 1:18) and renders visible the one no one has ever seen—this is what priests are called to be in their turn by virtue of the priestly character. Their mission as heralds of the Word rests upon the same foundation, upon the Father's self-revelation imprinted upon their own human selves.[6]

If the Middle Ages was a great period of faith, much of what followed undid the good wrought by scholastic philoso-

---

5 *Ibid.*, 202.
6 *Ibid.*, 204.

phy, and this is especially true in the priesthood. Many scholars believe that apart from the formative centuries of the Church's early life, no period is more critical to a study of Holy Orders than the sixteenth; this, because of the work of the Reformers, and even more for the pronouncement of the Council of Trent, the high point of the Counter-Reformation.

For decades prior to the outbreak of the Reformation, there had been continuing calls for reform from within the Church. At the heart of these pleas was the need among the faithful to be led by well-trained, holy, spiritual leaders. We had fallen into a period when theological education among the clergy, and knowledge of the faith among the laity was exceptionally weak. There was a general ignorance of Latin, catechesis was poor, attendance at Mass perfunctory, the Sacrament of Penance administered only infrequently, and superstition widespread. Large numbers of the clergy were living a lifestyle totally inconsistent with their commitment to celibacy—often in open relationships with women; they refused to dress clerically, did not frequent the sacraments themselves, some not even remembering the form for sacramental absolution when called on to administer it. Added to this, was the practice of buying and selling indulgences, popularized by the Dominican Johann Tetzel. As a protest to this, a young Augustinian professor named Martin Luther wrote his Archbishop:

> Papal indulgences for the building of Saint Peter's are being hawked about under your illustrious sanction. I regret that the faithful have conceived some erroneous notions about them. These unhappy souls believe if they buy a letter of pardon they are sure of their salvation.[7]

On October 31, 1517, he nailed his ninety-five theses to the door of the Wittenburg Cathedral, and publicly announced he

---

[7] John Dolan, "Martin Luther," *New Catholic Encyclopedia* (New York: McGraw Hill, 1967), VIII, 1087, cited in Patrick J. Dunn, *Priesthood* (New York: Alba House, 1990), 89.

was holding a debate on the value of indulgences, so that people might be enlightened as to their true worth, and the way they were being bantered about for personal financial gain. Such, of course, was only the tip of the iceberg, and it rapidly became apparent that Luther's ideas on the Church and the sacraments were quite radical. After many attempts to persuade Luther to modify his views, Pope Leo X, on June 15, 1520, issued a Bull of Excommunication, *Exsurge Domine*, in Rome, and Luther replied with a number of treatises written during the same year.

His *Appeal to the Christian Nobility of the German Nation* was especially peculiar in its lack of distinction between clergy and laity. If a large number of people were stranded on a desert island, he noted, and the majority of them selected one of their number to be a priest, such a one would as validly possess the office as if he had been ordained by the Pope. His argument was a priesthood of the faithful—all were priests in virtue of their Baptism, and all could, therefore, potentially exercise priestly functions. It followed that there was no such thing as a priestly character as the Church understood it; those who ministered as priests were simply those who had been appointed by the community, and as such, they could leave their priestly office at any time, and would no longer be considered priests.

Luther's *Babylonian Captivity of the Church* was far more radical, such that the philosopher Erasmus, after reading it, believed it precluded any possible chance for reconciliation with Rome. He considered the Church's seven sacraments, and concluded that only three—Baptism, Penance and the Eucharist— had actually been instituted by Christ. Scripture occupied a central place in his theology, but this was an interpretation of Scripture which disregarded previous study by the Fathers of the Church. Rather, he looked for the literal sense of every text in its original language, be it Greek or Hebrew. Therefore, when he considered such a thing as Church teaching on the Eucharist, he rejected transubstantiation as an improper expression of the mystery: its explanation, he felt, was too scholastic and not firmly based on Scripture. Further, he could not accept the Mass as a sacrifice, which, *ex opere operato*, could remit the sins of the living and the dead. This totally went against his concept of justification by faith alone. Instead, the Mass was merely a "proclamation of the death of Christ," in which all the baptized shared equally, an event which called forth faith on the part of all participants. If they were led by a particular individual, that person was one who was merely selected from all the believers, and any recognizable "ordination" rite of such persons signified the community's delegation and approval.

If the Mass is no longer a sacrifice, the notion of priests offering private Masses is completely superfluous, and, as might be expected, Luther strongly attacked it. Only the priestly community of believers could validly come together for a Eucharistic service of praise and thanksgiving proclaimed in faith, and, since this was its true meaning, what need was there to have the rite proclaimed in Latin? With the gradual movement toward the vernacular, Luther introduced a German "Mass"—the first such liturgy of the Reformation—at Wittenburg Cathedral on Christmas night, 1525. It was a Eucharistic service practically reduced to preaching, instruction, and admonition. Rather than a Catholic emphasis on the action of a priest-celebrant who confected the species of bread and wine and offered them to the Heavenly Father, people's attention was focused on little more than a communion service. Luther's intent was purposeful: Catholics at this time rarely received Holy Communion more than once a year, usually on one major feast. The gifts of God, he contended, were to be given to people more frequently.

The Church necessarily had to respond with one voice to this, and did so at the Council of Trent, the highlight of the Counter-Reformation. Many topics were addressed, many areas of faith strongly affirmed. Both the priesthood and the Eucharist received considerable treatment, and with the former, the Council Fathers were very clear on the "cultic" nature of the ordained priesthood. At the same time, the practice of priests saying Mass privately was not only defended, but actually encouraged:

> The Holy Council... does not condemn as illicit those Masses in which the priest alone communicates sacramentally, but rather approves and commends them... because they are celebrated by a public minister of the Church.[8]

It is the opinion of scholars of the Council that its most important statement in its Decree on the Sacrament of Order is its opening clause:

> *Sacrificium et sacerdotium ita Dei ordinatione coniuncta sunt...* (Sacrifice and priesthood are thus conjoined by divine ordinance).[9]

The "divine ordinance" linking the priesthood to its essential component of sacrifice involved the power to offer the accidents of bread and wine to the Father, consecrate them into the substance of the body and blood of Christ, and administer them to the faithful. Also tied to this is the power of forgiveness of sins, since it flows from the same sacrificial death made present in the same Eucharistic sacrifice. Priests who have this awesome power, the Council said, do not have it by a vote of the community. They have it from God, through the hands of an ordaining prelate, impressing on their souls an indelible character: making them not mere functionaries who can walk away at whim, but other Christs, uniquely configured to the Master.

Trent also strongly affirmed the sacrificial reality of the Mass and said it could only be understood in light of redemption, which is accomplished solely through the cross. Traditional Catholic belief in the Mass as the unbloody sacrifice of Calvary

---

[8] H.J. Schroeder, O.P., ed., *Canons and Decrees of the Council of Trent* (London: B. Herder Book Co., 1941), 147, cited in *Ibid.*, 94.

[9] Schroeder, 432, cited in *Ibid.*

comes from this Council, when the Fathers reminded all that the same Christ who had died on the cross is immolated again in the Mass—only the method of offering is different. The fruits of Christ's sacrificial death are obtainable in every Mass, to all those who approach the Lord "with a true heart and with upright faith, with fear and reverence, contrite and penitent." In addition, Luther's denial of transubstantiation was condemned, and Catholic belief reaffirmed:

> This Holy Council declares it anew, that by the consecration of the bread and wine a change is brought about of the whole substance.[10]

Such has remained the consistent teaching of the Church on the priestly character through the centuries. In 1949, the Archbishop of Paris, Emmanuel Cardinal Suhard, wrote a magnificent pastoral letter to his clergy titled *Priests Among Men*. It has become a classic study of the priesthood. In noting the special character of priests, Suhard was very clear that a priest "… must not be set in opposition to the faithful, as though the latter had nothing in common with him." On the other hand, such a man "… is not merely a baptized person. He is not a lay person vested with a temporary function, but a man set apart from the faithful, endowed by God with transcendent powers and marked with a consecratory character which sets him apart." This character, said the Cardinal, is distinguishable from the character of the baptized and confirmed in that it bestows on those who receive it "… the capacity of representing the sole Pontiff and acting in His name, in His stead."[11]

Less than two decades after Cardinal Suhard penned his letter, the Second Vatican Council spoke to the Church, the People of God in the modern world, with its Decree on the Life

---

[10] Schroeder, 75, cited in *Ibid.*, 95.
[11] Emmanuel Cardinal Suhard, *Priests Among Men* (New York: Integrity, 1949), 15-16.

and Ministry of Priests, *Presbyterorum Ordinis.* They describe priests as men set apart in a certain sense within the midst of God's people, not so they may be separated, but that they might be totally dedicated to the work for which the Lord has raised them up. Their office presupposes the sacraments of Baptism and Confirmation, but is itself a special sacrament:

> [T]he sacerdotal office of priests is conferred by that special sacrament through which priests, by the anointing of the Holy Spirit, are marked with a special character and are so configured to Christ the Priest that they can act in the person of Christ the Head.[12]

Hence, priests are called upon to be perfect as Christ's Heavenly Father is perfect. Christ has a special claim on them, as it were, since they have been consecrated to Him in a new way:

> To the acquisition of this perfection, priests are bound by a special claim since they have been consecrated to God in a new way by the reception of Orders. They have become living instruments of Christ the eternal priest, so that through the ages they can accomplish His wonderful work of reuniting the whole society of men with heavenly power.[13]

---

[12] *Presbyterorum Ordinis* (Decree on the Life and Ministry of Priests) I:2, in Walter M. Abbott, S.J., ed., *The Documents of Vatican II* (New York: Herder and Herder, 1966), 535.

[13] *Presbyterorum Ordinis* III:12, in *Ibid.*, 558.

6

The Eucharist and the Priesthood

"If everything in our Lord's life led up to Calvary," the respected French writer Bossuet observed, "then everything in a priest's life leads up to the Mass."[1] He was making the point that the sacrament and sacrifice of the Mass, the very mystery of our faith, must be the highlight and spiritual summit of every priest's day. He must engage his mind and heart in preparation for it, lest he fall into the category Saint John Chrysostom described when he wrote that the barking of dogs was more preferable to the Lord than priestly prayers offered halfheartedly. On the other hand, for any priest who seriously meditated on his sacred trust, great benefits could accrue. Dom Hubert Van Zeller explains:

> In England our cathedrals are fronted and flanked by lawns of cut grass which are called a "close." The town is kept at bay; there is no traffic across the close. The priest must contrive to lay down a "close" round his Mass: no traffic, no business before and after Mass— silence. The alternative is spiritual suffocation. With the Eucharistic part of his day safeguarded and allowed to give impetus to his charity, the priest will be able to meet the demands made upon him by his parish, by

---

[1] Cited in Dom Hubert Van Zeller, *The Gospel Priesthood* (New York: Sheed and Ward, 1956), 41.

his studies, by his correspondence. Steeped in the spirit of his Mass he will be able to take the Mass with him into his work.[2]

Not only the Mass, but especially the gift of the Eucharist in the Mass. The Eucharistic mystery is completed by the priest's reception of Holy Communion, where, as Saint Augustine notes, Christ becomes closer to us than we are to ourselves. Just as Old Testament priests were called to holiness of life, and physically nourished by the immolated victim they had offered in the Temple, so the priest of the new dispensation is called to a far greater business—to be another Christ. To achieve this, he is nourished not by a sacrificial lamb, but by the Lamb of God, slain for the world's redemption. The results are compelling:

> In Holy Communion there is a meeting of intellects. Christ's lucid intellect and our own obscured and confused; a meeting of wills, Christ's will confirmed in goodness and our own wavering and volatile; a meeting of sense powers, Christ's faculties detached from all that is sinful, and our own so often disordered and earthy.[3]

Father Jean Jacques Olier, founder of the Society of Saint Sulpice, saw the priest's reception of Holy Communion as a deep relationship with Christ's victimhood. He drew a comparison between the closeness of human beings with the food they eat and the Eucharistic food received by the priest in Holy Mass, and noted that in the first instance, the human being assimilates what he consumes: in the second, the priest is absolutely changed by what he consumes. As such, the priest must become a real victim with Christ, accepting all the Lord asks of him in the priesthood:

---

[2]   *Ibid.*, 45.

[3]   Rev. R. Garrigou-Lagrange, O.P., *The Priest in Union with Christ* (Cork: The Mercier Press Limited, 1951), 75-76.

Every priest should be a victim or a genuine host, by accepting whatever God has willed or permitted for his sanctification: in this way he is assimilated to Christ and works with Him, in Him, and through Him, for the saving of souls.... Our Saviour, by making use of bread and wine in Holy Communion, wishes to show that the priest and the host must be one and the same, that all priests should be real victims, and that just as they are God's priests only in and by Jesus Christ whose spirit dwells within them, so also must they become victims in union with Him and always continue in that state, if they want to be genuine priests like Himself.[4]

Nothing, it would seem, more clearly identifies the priesthood than the Eucharist, the real presence of the body, blood, soul and divinity of Jesus Christ, and the very special relationship each priest shares in bringing this mystery to himself and the people he serves. A prototype of this mystery was found in the Old Testament: when Saint John in his Gospel refers to Our Lord as the bread of life and the light of the world, he saw the Eucharistic presence of Christ as the fulfillment of two important symbols found in Jewish temples: a lampstand, and a table on which was placed what the Jews called the bread of presence.

Our Lord made reference to this when He spoke of "the loaves set out there before the Lord" (Matthew 12:4). There were twelve loaves, representing the twelve tribes of Israel, placed on a table and signifying the presence of the faithful with God at all times. One spiritual writer noted that if the Bread of Presence was the people's continual being with the Lord, the bread of the New Testament is the Lord's continual presence with His people. In Judaic times, God's people were always in His sight; with the dwelling of the Eucharistic Christ in our tabernacles, God's presence with His people is even more real, and through

---

[4] Cited in *Ibid.*, 77.

this marvelous gift, Saint Paul could describe the Church's one-ness, so reminiscent of the oneness of the twelve tribes of Israel:

> When we break the bread, is it not a means of sharing in the body of Christ? Because there is one loaf, we, many as we are, are one body; for it is one loaf of which we all partake.[5]

There is yet another parallel: the Book of Leviticus notes that "never must the altar be empty of this perpetual fire" (6:13). The reference is to a type of sanctuary lamp always kept burning before the Bread of Presence, a clear indication of God's presence with His people. Spiritual writers have seen a real foreshadowing of the Bread of Life, and to this day, the sanctuary lamp is kept burning in our churches pointing to His real presence.

The Old Testament is also a wonderful point of reference for concentrating on the gift of the Holy Eucharist in the life of a priest. In the sixth chapter of Saint John's Gospel, we read a lengthy discourse of Our Lord in which He compares and contrasts the feeding of the Israelites with manna in the desert wilderness, with the feeding of His faithful, priests and laity, in the Holy Eucharist. The manna, of course, is a type or shadow which is destined to disappear in the full light of the Gospel dispensation; it is simply a preparation for what is to be the greatest miracle of all, Christ's giving the gift of Himself in the great sacrament of His love.

God's gift of manna was only for a select number, His chosen ones who were to make the long, arduous journey from Egypt to the promised land. It was not given indiscriminately to any and all who just happened to be wayfaring through the desert. Rather, it fell in very close proximity to the dwellings of those who would need it. Meditating on this point in a retreat to priests some decades ago, Monsignor Ronald Knox wrote that

---

[5] 1 Corinthians 10:14.

"every exclusion implies an inclusion… the manna, in defining the Israelites and separating them from their fellow men united them more surely together, [and] gave them a corporate sense."[6] There was, then, a certain unity among God's chosen people, something which made them quite unique.

Curious that some began to complain against God's gift; at least it indicates the urgency of physical sustenance—the food was not a delicacy, it was a necessity. It began to fall just as the Israelites left Egypt, and had to be gathered each day and preserved, lest it deteriorate. A treat it was not; it was a miracle God repeated day after day of the forty-year journey:

> God doesn't ordinarily cheapen His miracles by making them into an everyday occurrence. Yet He did repeat this miracle of the manna; why? Perhaps because He wanted us to see clearly that the Holy Eucharist is meant to be our daily bread.[7]

The daily gathering up of God's gift was not limited to a select few; each member of the People of God had to do his or her share. Inevitably, some would gather more, some less. The miraculous fact is that each gathered what was completely sufficient to his or her needs, no more, no less. This sufficiency has traditionally been viewed as yet another foreshadowing of the Holy Eucharist in that the Lord's body, worthily received, provides us complete sufficiency in our journey to our heavenly homeland. In the life of every priest, the Eucharist satisfies all the hungerings, needs, and desires of his very human priestly heart.

The priest is, therefore, inserted into the mystery of the Holy Eucharist, sacrifice and sacrament, in a very unique way. The Eucharistic sacrifice which he offers is composed of the Liturgy of the Word and the Liturgy of the Eucharist, or, in older parlance, the Mass of the Catechumens and the Mass of the

---

6 Ronald Knox, *A Retreat for Priests* (London: Sheed and Ward, 1946), 78.
7 *Ibid.*, 80.

Faithful. It is the latter which radically distinguishes his priesthood, and identifies his configuration to Christ the High Priest. Avery Cardinal Dulles, in his work, *The Priestly Office*, reflects on the nature of this Eucharistic sacrifice and observes that most of the prayers the priest says are expressed in the first person plural. The acknowledgment that we come before the Lord to seek his forgiveness, the Gloria, the Creed, etc., are recited together in this collective sense. It is not until the actual words of consecration, Our Lord's very words of institution, that the first person singular is used. If this were not the case, the mystery could not be made present for us. If the past tense and indirect discourse were used, merely informing believers that Our Lord had commanded His disciples they should carry this out, it would be religious ritual devoid of any meaning—Christ would not be truly present. The Cardinal also cites scholarly opinion other than his own to reinforce the idea that were the tense otherwise, what happened at the Last Supper would not be allowed to happen again. Speaking as he does *"in persona Christi,"* says Dulles, the priest allows Christ to speak through him, making the Lord's sacrifice just as really and truly present. Such is reminiscent of Saint John Chrysostom's teaching on the priest lending his tongue and giving his hand to Christ; such words, of course, only effecting what they signify when the one uttering them has been validly ordained to act in the person of Christ the Head:

> Sacramental ordination to priestly office confers the power to pronounce the words of consecration in such a way that Christ is the principal speaker and actor. Only in this way is it possible for the Eucharist to be identically the same sacrifice that was offered on Calvary. As the Council of Trent clearly taught, the priest and the victim are the same; only the manner of offering is different.[8]

---

[8]   Avery Dulles, S.J., *The Priestly Office: A Theological Reflection* (New York: Paulist Press, 1997), 39-40.

This idea of every priest as both a priest and a victim in the Eucharistic sacrifice was beautifully developed by the late Archbishop Fulton J. Sheen in his many retreats to priests in the United States and Europe:

> Some things are too beautiful to be forgotten. Memorial Day recalls the sacrifices of soldiers for their country. Arnold Toynbee reminds us: "We have roses in June that we may have memories in December." Our Blessed Lord came not to live, but to die. He would not, therefore, leave to the chance recollection of men the memory of His Victimhood. He Himself would institute the precise means of its recall. This He did at the Last Supper: "Do this as a memorial of Me" (1 Corinthians 11:24).[9]

A memorial is a recalling of a past event worthy of remembering. For example, each year the Jews came together for their annual observance of Passover, the celebration of the meal in which they ate the victim lamb sacrificed in the Temple. They were recalling a past event—what God had done for their ancestors so many generations before in allowing them to escape captivity and journey to the promised land. What is important to remember is that the Jews were doing more than merely recollecting the past—to them, the celebration of Passover was also a present reality, the events of the past brought into the present moment. Such was to be the case with the new Passover that Our Lord instituted, with one significant addition: it was also to be one which looked to the future, since Christ commanded His Apostles to repeat it once He was risen:

> Suppose a Greek drama of Aeschylus was enacted on the Athenian stage. The purpose of drama, according to Aristotle, is to purge the soul. When the crowds left the theater bettered in soul and conscious of guilt, they

---

9 Fulton J. Sheen, *Those Mysterious Priests* (Garden City, NY: Doubleday, 1974), 147.

said to one another, "What a shame that this tragedy is performed only once. Everyone in the world should see it; their characters would be so enobled." But how could that be done? By keeping the same lines and the same plot, but using different actors and sending the show throughout the world.[10]

Archbishop Sheen, whose cause for sainthood has been officially opened, described the Mass as Calvary put into space and time through the action of priests, other Christs, functioning in each generation. In many of his conferences to priests, and days of recollection for lay people, he invariably described the Mass as a drama in three acts: Offertory, Consecration and Communion. Every drama first had to be conceived in the mind of its author, the cast of characters carefully chosen, rehearsals dutifully conducted, a grand opening night performance at a given locale, followed by scores of actors taking the performance on the road. The Mass, said Sheen, could be similarly conceived. Our Lord had prepared the paschal mystery from all eternity, chosen His Twelve Apostles very specifically, had His "opening night" at the Last Supper where he commissioned the Twelve to perform the mystery in memory of Him, and those Twelve subsequently ordained others who would bring the mystery of faith to the entire world. The Archbishop traced the origin of this mystery to the Book of Revelation, which speaks of "the lamb that was slain since the foundation of the world":

> The drama of Redemption was historically enacted at Calvary. The Lord foreseeing it on Thursday night, arranged that the Memorial of His Redemption should be made available to the world. He made the priests the first road company, and ever since then, other road companies are saying the same lines, renewing the same mystery in every part of the world. In the Mass, the Cross is lifted out of rocky Calvary and planted in

---

[10] *Ibid.*, 147-148.

Nairobi, Tokyo, Athens and Moscow. Everyone in the world may now not only see it, but relive it. Only sensible advantages would accrue to those who wished they had been at Calvary and the empty tomb. The same drama is repeated in the Mass and faith interprets the event in both instances.[11]

When Our Lord told His Apostles to "do this," the verb translated from Greek is plural, indicating it was to be done over and again—the mystery unfolded in the Upper Room and on Calvary was to continue for all time; on Calvary the offering was the shedding of Christ's blood, in the Mass the manner is unbloody, though it is the same death and resurrection:

> In the Mass we offer ourselves to Christ in the consecration; we die with Christ. Suppose Christ has no Resurrection; then we would be dissolved into His death and that would be the end. But Easter follows Good Friday. We die to live again. At the moment of Communion, Christ says to us: You have given Me your death; I will now give you My Life. You have given Me your time; I will give you My Eternity. You gave Me your nothingness; I will give you My All.[12]

The effects of Holy Communion on the priest are tremendous; Saint John spoke of the Bread of Life in the sixth chapter of his Gospel, and Saint Paul, writing to the early Christians of Corinth, taught that each time one received the Lord's body and blood, he proclaimed the death of that same Lord. Hence, the priest is assimilated into Christ's life and death in a profoundly mysterious fashion that he, in his human imperfection, will not even remotely comprehend this side of eternity.

Dom Columba Marmion was yet another commentator who meditated on how the spiritual effects of the Eucharist

---

[11] *Ibid.*, 148.
[12] *Ibid.*, 156.

strengthened the priest-victim who offers and is offered with Christ in every Eucharistic sacrifice. In one of his retreats to priests, he considered the parable of the wedding banquet found in both Matthew and Luke's Gospels. The King is the Heavenly Father; when He planned from all eternity that His Son would assume a human nature, He was, in fact, preparing a great nuptial feast, symbolized by the hypostatic union of Our Lord—the joining of two natures, human and divine in one divine person. Borrowing Saint Gregory the Great's thought that this hypostatic union symbolized, in a mystical way, the union of Christ with His Church, Marmion adds that by so uniting Himself, Christ was entering every human soul through sanctifying grace and charity.

Many, of course, excused themselves from the wedding feast, claiming other duties of importance. The King then commanded His servants to go into the streets and byways, inviting all who would come, a great foreshadowing of the call to all Christian peoples to the Eucharistic banquet, to share in its countless riches. Once again relying on authors like Origen and Saint Jerome, Marmion explained to priests that those who avail themselves of the banquet truly share in the union of love initiated by Christ, who takes possession of their souls, and bestows on them the fruits of redemption. This greatest of all the world's love stories is brought to completion with the effects of Holy Communion in every priest:

> Corporal food is first absorbed; the organism then assimilates it to itself and in this way it conserves life and encourages growth. The Eucharistic bread operates in us in an analogous manner. While we receive it with our mouths, *quod ore sumpsimus*, Christ unites Himself to the soul; *pura mente capiamus*. He fecundates and increases in the soul the divine life of which Baptism has bestowed the seed. The individual changes ordinary food into his own substance; but in receiving the Eucharist we do not change Jesus Christ into ourselves.

On the contrary, it is He, the food of life, who transforms us into Himself. In the mystery of this union, we see verified the mysterious words which Saint Augustine puts on the lips of the Lord: "I am the food of grown men; grow and you shall eat Me. And you shall not change Me into yourself as bodily food, but into Me you shall be changed." This is the first sacramental effect, *ex opere operato,* of Holy Communion worthily received....[13]

Such is a transforming union which, ever so gradually, allows the priest to be transformed into the object of His love. There is not a single virtue known in the Christian dispensation that is not brought to life, and, if the priest acts upon them, the results will clearly show in the way he interacts with the people he is sent to serve. Additionally, he will experience the effect of inner spiritual joy—not necessarily a joy felt on the emotional level, since sentiment is not to be confused with reality, and human nature seldom allows one to live purely on a sentimental level. The inner spiritual joy of the Eucharist is the joy of faith, and the conscious act of a priestly will which has freely chosen to love and serve the Eternal High Priest:

> The Father requires us to reproduce in ourselves the characteristics of His Son Incarnate; we must become so like Christ that the Father will recognize us as His true children. The Eucharist is a potent support to us in this work of assimilation to Christ; it confers on us the necessary graces to conform in all things to Jesus by accepting the divine will, by giving ourselves to our neighbor, by patience and by pardon. We all want to be fervent priests. We may be weak by temperament, or perhaps energetic, but to all this sacrament communicates the strength which comes from God.[14]

---

[13] Dom Columba Marmion, O.S.B., *Christ—The Ideal of the Priest* (London: Sands & Co. Publishers, Ltd., 1952), 215-216.

[14] *Ibid.,* 216.

7

Suffering and Prayer,
Essential Ingredients of the Priesthood

The taking up of the cross never has been, nor could it ever be, foreign to the priestly life. In fact, it is one of the essential ingredients:

> The priest may not be departmental in his relationship to Christ and Christ's members. He cannot choose to follow Christ in His preaching but not in His suffering, to worship His Incarnation but neglect His act of Redemption, to preach His Transfiguration and not to practice His doctrine of the Cross, to follow Him in His charity but not in His Gethsemani. The disciple must be as his master, the servant as his lord. If Christ is the Divine Mediator, the priest is the divinely appointed human mediator.[1]

The place Christ occupies in any priest's life is the very reason for his priestly existence. Christ our High Priest, who suffered for all humanity, molds and configures every man who shares His priesthood, and this process is nothing less than a share in His suffering, and an invitation to the life of prayer.

---

[1] Dom Hubert Van Zeller, O.S.B., *The Gospel Priesthood* (New York: Sheed and Ward, 1956), 23.

These are two courses one must take in the school of purification, as the priest constantly strives for a greater purity of heart. The late Basil Cardinal Hume of Westminster, England, speaking to his priests, and through his writings to all priests, lays great stress on each priest's learning to embrace the cross which the Lord has specifically fitted to his shoulders. He can do it to the extent he meditates on the admonition found in the rite of Ordination, to "pattern your life on the mystery of the Lord's cross." He can do it to the extent he realizes the cross given him is usually not the one which would be to his personal liking; it is not the one which will be timed perfectly so as not to interfere with the rest of his life; it is not the one which will necessarily be dramatic and short-lived—more often it will be the ongoing, daily, continuous trials and difficulties of life. Finally, he can do it to the extent he knows that by such crosses, the Lord is trying to detach him from what is unimportant in his life, so that his love might increase, not through the gift of immediate spiritual consolation or emotional highs, but by the perseverance of daily fidelity. It is only in this way that the priest will ever hear the inner voice of the Lord asking, "Do you love me?", and be able to reply with a resounding yes.

Each criticism, disappointment, harsh word, frustration, etc., a priest experiences in the course of daily living is part of his individual cross. Many, perhaps far too many, are slow to learn from the particulars the Lord sends them. Some may even be tempted to ask "why suffering?" Others, observing the priesthood from outside, could possibly ask why anyone would consider such a way of life. In trying to answer that, Cardinal Hume noted that suffering in any form not only purifies us, but compels us to ask basic, fundamental questions about life, and provides us at least some solutions. Far from avoiding priestly adversities, the ordained man should get down on his knees and thank the Lord for whatever cross He has sent us. Writing as a priest of forty years, the Cardinal admitted he had succeeded in doing that only once, but the one instance had made such a forceful impact on his life he had never forgotten it. Also, he felt there was a side to every priest which did welcome suffering; a side which realized that just as the Lord shared in all aspects of our humanity, save sin, so we must expect to similarly share in all of His, including His passion and death:

> Because when I am suffering, whether it is mental or physical, whether in union with Our Lord in His agony in the garden or in union with Him as He is actually carrying the burden, being flogged and spat upon, going up the hill to Calvary—there is nothing that brings us closer to Our Lord, and through Him to the Father than actually suffering with Him.[2]

Each priest has the consolation of knowing that his share in Christ's sufferings is not unique to his particular vocation; every soul in the world who has taken the following of Christ seriously has embraced the cross, and with all of them the priest enjoys a great solidarity. If one may speak of the vocation of suffering being accepted in life situations in any order of priority, the priesthood would be high on the list, if not first: it would be extremely difficult for a man to speak to people about faith if he has never struggled with doubt; to speak to them about suffering if he has not undergone his own; to encourage them to see the light if he has not experienced his own darkness. In fact, it is entirely possible that a man who has been given great responsibility will bear a cross of similar proportion.

There is a story often told of Pope Paul VI when he was Archbishop of Milan. An artist had made him a very beautiful crucifix for the chapel of his residence, but the crucifix had no crown of thorns. When the then Archbishop Montini commented on this to the artist, he responded that this was the way things were supposed to be, since the Lord had given a very specific crown of thorns to the Archbishop of Milan. Interestingly, the same Archbishop, some years later when he had become Pope, received Archbishop Fulton J. Sheen in private au-

---

[2] Basil Hume, O.S.B., *Light in the Lord* (Middlegreen, Slough: ST PAULS Publications, 1991), 132.

dience. The American prelate commented that the Pontiff had been well named Paul since, in imitation of the Apostle to the Gentiles, he had been stoned by his own within the household of the faith. The Pope replied how true that statement was, noting that each day when he opened his mail, a crown of thorns could be found in at least one piece of correspondence, if not many. But, said the Pope, it gave him an indescribable joy to know that he was, in the words of his namesake, filling up in his own flesh what was lacking to the passion of Christ for the sake of His body, the Church.

The Pope's reference to Saint Paul's Letter to the Colossians (1:24) makes it clear that all Christians may unite their sufferings with the ongoing passion of Christ. In the life of the priest, this is tremendously important, and, said Saint Augustine, it is not something the priest should be surprised at. As members of the Body of Him whose head was crowned with thorns, all must expect to share in His suffering. In the fourth century, this had particular poignancy, since the Church had emerged from an Old Testament tradition in which the priest, the holy man, was seen only as an offerer of sacrifice, as one who stood at the altar and interceded for God's people; he was not seen as part of the sacrifice itself. In the Christian priesthood, this division no longer exists:

> The man who celebrates Mass is, mystically and figuratively but nonetheless significantly, on the paten at the *Suspice* and in the chalice at the *Offerimus*. It would be a mistake to think of our Mass and our position in it as separated into parts: I, the man, as the subject; the sacred species, the material element, as the object; God, Father, Son and Holy Ghost, as the end. But because Christ is at once priest, victim, and end of His own sacrifice, so we can think of ourselves, made one with Christ in His sacrificial act, as directed towards the same Father in the same redemptive act.[3]

---

[3]   Van Zeller, *op. cit.*, 17-18.

Not only does the priest share in the passion of Christ, he is in fact continuing that same passion. The Letter to the Colossians demonstrates this in at least two ways:

> (1) That a Christian's sufferings share in the sufferings of Christ, because the Christian and Christ are somehow one. (2) There is a quota of suffering that is assigned to the Church, the corporate Christ, in order to complete God's plan for salvation. "Christ's afflictions" include His historical agony in His physical body, which we are: Christ's quota has been fulfilled, but not the Church's quota. What the Church endures until the end of time, and what Israel suffered before Christ in anticipation both enters into Him.[4]

This truth is also found in the Acts of the Apostles (26:14). Saul, the great persecutor of Christianity, is confronted on the Damascus road and asked by the Lord why he is persecuting Him. It is very noteworthy that Christ did not say why are you persecuting My Church; rather the persecution was directed to the Lord Jesus Himself, since His presence in the world was no longer a physical one, but He was mystically present in all His members. Saul was persecuting the body of Christ, so the head of the body, Christ in heaven, complained. The agony of His physical body had ended; the agony of His mystical body was continuing. Paul's starting point was the cross; he then had to retrace his steps to Calvary:

> The Passion endures through history something like a volcano. The peak of the volcano emits fire and lava, but in its depths are ageless fires which are like the "Lamb slain, as it were, from the beginning of the world...."[5]

---

[4] Fulton J. Sheen, *Those Mysterious Priests* (Garden City, NY: Doubleday, 1979), 107.
[5] *Ibid.*, 109.

The passion of Christ continues in a conscious way in the life of every priest. Consciously, whenever he unites any trial to those of Christ, the passion is present. Unconsciously, in the loneliness he experiences with the rest of humanity, the passion is equally present. In whichever manner the cross is present in the priestly life, it can never be experienced in a vacuum—on one's own, apart from the rest of the world. Such would be wasted pain, futile and devoid of sense. What makes suffering fruitful is joining it to a life of prayer:

> There comes a point when one is overburdened and hurting, when the only prayer that is possible is the prayer of Our Lord on the Cross, "My God, my God, why have you forsaken me?" You can find an extraordinary peace, I believe in sharing that experience of the Lord. When prayer in the verbal sense, in the sense of using my mind, does not come easily, what better prayer than to take the crucifix and just look at it and allow it to give you something of its secret. If you are sharing the experience of the Lord in some manner, then it reveals to you something of the secret. Whatever that secret says to you can bring you its own peace, its own joy.[6]

Suffering and prayer are, therefore, the essential ingredients of the priestly life, and this combination opens up the larger question of the place of prayer in the life of every priest. Decades ago, Blessed Columba Marmion, in his retreat conference to priests, stressed that prayer was the way one ascended to the Lord. This could be done in one of three ways: by contemplating the created world and the beauties of God's nature which surround us, by meditating on God's revealed truths as they are found in the pages of Scripture, or by attaching oneself to Christ with the liveliest of faith, and allowing oneself to be totally led by Christ. Each priest was perfectly free to choose any of these

---

[6]   Hume, *op. cit.*, 135.

three methods, depending on his temperament, personality, and the circumstances of his life. Marmion offered a unique comparison between the priest's life of prayer and the Temple of Jerusalem, describing each of the courtyards as they increased in dignity the closer they were to the holy of holies:

> The courtyard of the Gentiles was a very broad, open space, unroofed. Everyone could enter it. From this courtyard one entered into that of the Jews through doors by which the uncircumcised could not pass. In this vast enclosure, the chosen people assisted at the sacrifices, heard the readings of the Law, and sang psalms. From here they could see, behind the altar of holocausts, that part of the sanctuary which was reserved for the ministers of religion. At the end of the place which was called Holy, behind the sacred veil of the Temple, *post velamentum*, came the mysterious Holy of Holies. There, according to the Epistle to the Hebrews (9:3-4), beside the altar of incense, was the ark of the testament, covered with gold, which contained the tables of the Law, the manna, and the rod of Aaron. Once a year, after many purifications, the high priest entered this sanctuary alone.[7]

The Court of the Gentiles symbolized that type of prayer in which a person is drawn to God not by the help of divine revelation, but through the direct contemplation of what he finds around him in the universe. Marmion specifically mentions the immensity of the ocean, the peaks of the mountains, and the majesty of the landscape. Such settings are marvelous inducements to prayer and advancement in the spiritual life, since behind what is so readily apparent and spectacularly beautiful, the hidden presence of God can be found.

---

[7]   Dom Columba Marmion, O.S.B., *Christ—The Ideal of the Priest* (London: Sands & Co. Publishers Ltd., 1952), 250.

In the Court of the Jews, we move to the supernatural level, to the order of revelation. The Mosaic worship with which the Jews were very familiar had been prescribed to Moses by God Himself. Likewise, in the priest's prayer it is just as important to listen very carefully to what God is saying through the words of the inspired text of Scripture. From a careful, thoughtful meditation on the words of Christ, much prayer can come into the priest's life, and from that prayer, insights, directions, and genuine growth in holiness. The priest begins to appreciate more fully the mysteries of Christ's life, and to apply their meaning to his own. Such is a splendid form of mental prayer for any ordained, one which the Church has long respected:

> In early times, learning mental prayer meant, primarily, acquiring the habit of pausing in the course of one's reading of the Holy Scripture or of a pious work. During these pauses, the soul meditated, reflected, convinced itself of the truths proposed, realized its duties, made acts of conformity to the divine will, and gave expression to its hopes and its petitions. When these sentiments of faith, confidence and love were exhausted, one resumed quite simply the reading of the sacred text. This was the approach to mental prayer as the Fathers of the desert, those great masters of holiness, understood it. With St. Benedict, the monks of the West simply carried on this tradition. St. Teresa of Avila also recommended this method. It is a very simple method, but it has the very great advantage of being within the capacity of everyone, and it lessens distractions. Considering that so many souls have been introduced to contemplation in the past by this way, why should it not lead us to this same grace?[8]

Finally, one approaches the Holy of Holies, that part of the Temple where only the high priest was permitted to enter, and

---

[8]   *Ibid.*, 253.

only once a year, to offer sacrifice and to pray for the people in a spirit of profound adoration. Marmion sees this as the priest's soul entering into the contemplation of pure faith, and describes it as the prayer of "simple consideration: one looks, loves and is silent." Such stages are found in the writings of many great spiritual masters, and Marmion in particular feels the attempt to make such a spiritual climb is absolutely vital in every priest's life. Ours must be a continuous striving, for in the end our prayer is the "reflection of the expression of the true state of the soul."

These thoughts, written long ago, serve to remind priests that as followers of Christ, configured to Him in a special way, and entrusted with the task of carrying on His work, what is most important is our personal loyalty and close friendship with Him. "What good does a medical convention achieve," Archbishop Fulton J. Sheen once asked, "if the doctors agree on the need for good health, but take no practical steps to implement their argument?"[9] On a practical level, Sheen lost no opportunity when giving priests' retreats to stress the need of a daily holy hour made in the presence of the Blessed Sacrament. His strong emphasis on this particular form of prayer had many reasons.

Primarily, it is time spent in the Lord's presence, and if our faith is strong, no other reason is really necessary. Life was, and is, very fast-paced for many priests, and the Archbishop noted we all have "noonday devils" that have to be shaken off. Only time spent alone with the Lord will do it. Perhaps the most compelling reason of all is that it is the only thing the Lord ever specifically asked of His followers—the spending of an hour with Him. Matthew's Gospel records the haunting question, and those priests who respond to it with sincerity and fervor will discover very fruitful results:

---

9   Fulton J. Sheen, *The Priest Is Not His Own* (New York: McGraw Hill Book Company, Inc., 1963), 227.

We begin by walking with Our Lord but our eyes are "held fast," so that we do not "recognize Him." Next, He converses with our soul, as we read the Scriptures. The third stage is one of sweet intimacy, as when "He sat down at table with them." The fourth stage is the full dawning of the mystery of the Eucharist. Our eyes are "opened" and we recognize Him. Finally we reach the point where we do not want to leave. The hour seemed so short.[10]

To these, Archbishop Sheen added other considerations. He stressed the thought of Saint Thomas Aquinas that any power the priest had over the faithful, Christ's mystical body, derived from the power he was given in ordination to consecrate Christ's physical body in the Holy Sacrifice of the Mass. Because he can confer the body and blood of the Lord, the priest may teach, govern and sanctify the Lord's members. Everything he does sacramentally flows from this awesome gift, be it sacramental, doctrinal or pastoral. All power resides in the tabernacle, and the more the priest tries to evade time spent in the presence of Christ, the less effective he will be.

The daily holy hour allows a priest to maintain the balance between the temporal and spiritual in a very frantic world; it also allows each man to regain an often easily lost spiritual vitality. At an even deeper level, Sheen stressed the revelations of the Heart of Christ to Saint Margaret Mary Alacoque at Paray-Le-Monial, France in 1673. Such revelations indicate unexplored depths of that Divine Heart to be penetrated, especially by priests. "There are veils of love behind which only the priest may penetrate," Sheen wrote, "and from which he will emerge with an unction and power over souls far beyond his own strength."[11]

The holy hour would also make the priest an "obedient

---

[10] *Ibid.*

[11] *Ibid.*, 229.

instrument of divinity." This is understood in the twofold effect of the Eucharist in the priest's life: there is a movement of the priestly heart to the Eucharistic heart; as a result of this, there is also a movement of that same priestly heart to the people. The priest becomes totally pliable in the hands of Christ, and he begins to see his true self much more clearly: not the priest the people see, but the inner man the priest knows himself to be. It is an hour which deepens a man's humility, gives him strength over temptation and human weakness, and allows him to realistically assess his spiritual progress. "Presenting ourselves before Our Lord in the Blessed Sacrament," the Archbishop wrote, "is like putting a tubercular patient in good air and sunlight. The virus of our sins cannot long exist in the face of the Light of the World."[12]

The holy hour should also be made because it is very personal prayer, as opposed to the public prayer of the Mass, and the Liturgy of the Hours. The priest who limits himself only to official prayers is much like the union man who "downs tools the moment the whistle blows." There is also a tremendous good accruing to the entire Church from the personal prayer of each priest—especially when he is concentrating his mental energies on praying for the general welfare of Christ's body.

Such reasons cannot help but compel the priest who takes his vocation seriously, especially in times when so much of our culture militates against all we stand for. It will work wonders for all priests who enter into it heart and soul. Put very practically, Basil Hume tells us what we may expect:

> There will come a moment, as you go quietly through your prayer, when you are just happy to be there, knowing God is present. I think it is an experience a lot of people have. It is a golden moment and when it happens it is a gift from God. He makes that moment happen, you do not. But it will not happen unless you

---

12 *Ibid.*, 232.

are there and trying to raise your mind and heart up to God. How often does that experience happen? It may be only once in forty years. What do I learn from it? I learn from it one of the most important principles of the spiritual life: I am there not to derive benefit for myself, I am there to do it, to give, to be present to God.[13]

---

[13] Hume, *op. cit.*, 122.

8

The Priest as Preacher of the Word of God

Joseph Cardinal Ratzinger, Prefect of the Sacred Congregation for the Doctrine of the Faith, situates the importance of the priestly role of preacher of God's word for the ordained of the twenty-first century:

> After the Council, the impression arose here and there that there were more urgent things to do than to proclaim the word of God and to administer the sacraments. Many were of the opinion that one first had to establish a different society before one could again devote time to such things. At the root of such views lay a spiritual blindness that was only able to perceive material values and forgot that men and women always need the whole, that both their physical and their spiritual hunger must be answered. Nor can spiritual questions be put off. On the contrary, their postponement or exclusion only incites other problems and makes them even more impossible to solve.[1]

The relationship between preaching and the priestly office takes us back to the earliest days of the Church. Saint Paul, in his Letter to the Romans, is very clear about it:

---

[1] Joseph Ratzinger, *Ministers of Your Joy* (Middlegreen, Slough: ST PAULS Publications, 1989), 90.

For every one who calls upon the name of the Lord will be saved. But how are men to call upon Him in whom they have not believed? And how are they to believe in Him of whom they have never heard? And how are they to hear without a preacher? And how can men preach unless they are sent?[2]

There must always be those whose task it is to tell people about God, so that they may know Him, love Him, and continually call upon Him. Christ Himself told His closest collaborators, the Apostles, that He had been sent by His heavenly Father to teach only what the Father had taught Him. The Second Vatican Council, in its Decree on the Life and Ministry of Priests, noted the development of Our Lord's words through the generations of His Church's life, and stated that all priests were co-workers with their bishops in the proclamation of God's word. The fullness of that word, the word of salvation, is found only in Christ's One, Holy, Catholic and Apostolic Church, and only she can teach it in its completeness. In carrying out this task, bishops and priests are doing nothing less than fulfilling the Lord's dictate to "Go, therefore, and make disciples of all nations... teaching them to observe all that I have commanded you."[3]

If we may speak in terms of a priest's "authority" to preach, it is only because he is configured in a unique way to Him who has supreme authority, and who said to His own Apostles, "As the Father has sent Me, so also I send you."[4] As Christ's priest, he has been sent to preach to everyone; Saint Mark, in his Gospel, lays great stress on the fact that not one person in the world is excluded from hearing the Good News. When one considers the percentage of the world's population who have never heard, the challenge takes on awesome proportions. The priest is given authority to preach God's word only; the whole of it, not merely

---

[2]   Romans 10:13-15.

[3]   Matthew 28:19-20.

[4]   John 20:21.

a portion which might be particularly soothing at a given moment in time. He is to preach it as it is; not as he feels it should be. He is to preach it with the authority of Christ, and nothing in his personal makeup, intellectual training, or powers of eloquent persuasion allows him to lay claim to such authority; only the call and command of the High Priest give legitimacy to the preacher's role.

The very real importance of the priest's commissioning is related in the sixth chapter of the Acts of the Apostles. In a reading traditionally proclaimed at diaconate ordinations, one reads of the Apostles discussing among themselves how their time might be more profitably spent; specifically, how they might engage themselves more completely in the ministry of the word and prayer. Their solution, after much prayer, was the selection of seven deacons who would, more properly, wait on table and carry out functions the Apostles previously had done. If the Apostles believed that preaching and prayer were important enough for them to delegate some of their responsibilities, the message for today's priest is very clear: preaching, and the prayer underlying it are to be integral components of his existence.

This idea is further enforced by Saint Paul in his First Letter to the early Christians at Corinth. Christ had sent him "not to baptize, but to preach the Gospel" (1:7). Such does not minimize Baptism; it emphasizes the fact that once baptized into Christ's life, the believer must work out his salvation. He cannot do this if he does not know the way; it must be preached to him so that the map of life is clearly charted. It is a message intended to fill the believer with hope, Paul reminded the Christians living at Ephesus, since it was "the message of truth, the Gospel of your salvation" (1:13).

The fact that the world looks elsewhere, as the message goes unheeded, or even ignored, should come as no surprise to any priest. After all, Saint Paul met with discouraging results in Athens; after considerable preaching on the Areopagus, his "spirit was provoked within him as he saw that the city was full of idols."[5] Similarly, the Second Vatican Council pointed out that the modern world, which has unlocked the secrets of so much of nature and the universe, and has made such tremendous strides in technology and medical science, still raises questions about a human being's ultimate worth in the scheme of things, as well as the final end of humanity. The priest's role as preacher is to provide those answers to all who will listen. He must remind his hearers (as the author of the *Didache*, that book of early Church teachings, reminded the early Christians) that the Lord is to be found wherever His word is present.

Through the centuries, a great deal has been written about the priest as preacher. In the sixth century, Pope Saint Gregory the Great wrote to priests that they must have the ministry of preaching constantly before their mind's eye, and take very seriously the Lord's admonition of teaching in His name until He comes. Gregorian scholars note that Gregory's use of the Latin verb *docere* (to teach), rather than *praedicare* (to preach), underscores his strong conviction that sacred eloquence is the most important form of Christian instruction. To this, Gregory added an important note: a priest must not only preach about matters sublime, he must manifest those same qualities in his personal life, and show by his conduct how deeply he believes what he preaches.

In the thirteenth century, Saint Thomas Aquinas took a more intellectual approach, setting out three specific criteria for all preachers:

> He who preaches the faith must speak in such a way that the word of God enlightens the intellect, gives spiritual delight to the affections, and effectively inspires the will to be obedient to the divine commands with the aid of grace.[6]

5   Acts 17:16.
6   Cited in R. Garrigou-Lagrange, O.P., *The Priest in Union with Christ* (Cork: The Mercier Press Ltd., 1951), 122.

Aquinas saw the fulfillment of these criteria in the preaching of Christ and the Apostles. In Our Lord's life, He taught the mysteries of the Kingdom, but, as spiritual writers are quick to note, though He taught with authority, His teaching was imparted with simplicity and great humility. He persuasively spoke to the emotions of all when He told them of His Father's love for them. In spite of the hostility of the scribes and Pharisees, many who never heard such teaching came to Him. His own Apostles, the first to hear, responded by the shedding of their blood.

Only absolute truth could inspire such apostolic witness, and the priest is charged with preaching that same truth, uncomfortable as it may be to some, unpopular as it may make the preacher. Saint Philip Neri, the sixteenth century founder of the Oratorians, insisted that preachers must present to the faithful the clear choice which is theirs: eternal happiness or eternal punishment. On one occasion, he reminded a working man, very preoccupied with making a living, that he must be equally, if not more, preoccupied with eternal life. More poignant was a conversation with a priest, whose sole concern appeared to be ecclesiastical prestige:

> "And now what do you desire?" "I would like to be an apostolic nuncio!" "Very well, but what then?" "Perhaps a cardinal." "But what then?" "Perhaps the Pope." "And then?" The priest replied: "That is a pointless question. There is nothing more after the Papacy." "I beg to differ," was St. Philip's reply, "there is something more—death. And after death there is either Purgatory and then Heaven or Hell. You would do far better to desire eternal life than a nunciature."[7]

The twenty-first century has witnessed a shying away from controversial topics on the part of some preachers. Many do not preach doctrine for fear of upsetting those who might become

---

[7] Cited in *Ibid.*, 135.

offended. This is especially true in the area of sexual morality. This misdirected pastoral sensitivity was addressed by Pope Benedict XV in 1917, and he has much to say to contemporary times in summarizing the contributions of Saint Paul, one of the greatest of preachers:

> He imparted all the teaching and precepts of Christ, even the most stern; he did not hold back or soften anything that concerned humility, self-denial, chastity, contempt for merely human things, obedience, forgiveness for enemies, and other such subjects. He showed no timidity in declaring that a choice must be made between the service of God and that of Belial, that one cannot serve both; that a fearful judgment awaits men after death; that there can be no compromising with God; one can hope for eternal life if the whole law be obeyed, but if one neglects duty by yielding to unlawful desires, then it is the punishment of eternal fire which is to be expected.[8]

Three years later, this same Pontiff wrote another encyclical to commemorate the fifteenth centenary of the death of Saint Jerome, the great Scripture scholar. In his letter *Spiritus Paraclitus*, Benedict considers the Scriptures indispensable for the priest's mission, as well as great nourishment for his spiritual life. As a source of inspiration for preaching, however, there was no substitute for God's word. In fact, an individual priest's words

> ...carry neither weight nor authority, nor have they any power to fashion men's souls, unless they are moulded by the Scriptures from which they draw force and power. For "everything that the Scripture says is like a mighty trumpet call that smites the ears of the

---

[8]   *Humani Generis*, cited in Pierre Veuillot (ed.), *The Catholic Priesthood: Papal Documents from Pius X to Pius XII* (Dublin: M.H. Gill and Son, Ltd., 1957), 116.

faithful with its warning message"; "nothing is so strik-
ing as an example from the Sacred Scriptures."[9]

In the years following the Second Vatican Council, the
ministry of the word has occupied much theological writing,
including such modern lights as Cardinals Hans Urs Von
Balthasar and Joseph Ratzinger. Von Balthasar relies heavily on
the themes of sending and obedience found in John's Gospel:
Christ's heavenly Father commanded Him what to say, sent
Him into the world to say it, and the Lord, in turn, commissioned His followers to do the same. In doing this, Our Lord is
seen as the Good Shepherd, constantly guarding His flock and
ultimately offering His life on the altar of the cross for them. The
preaching and teaching of every priest, says the Swiss theologian, is always done in imitation of that Shepherd.

Von Balthasar is joined by Cardinal Joseph Ratzinger in
his strong emphasis on preaching. The word which every priest
is charged with, says the Cardinal Prefect, is one which comes
from above. It is passed from one generation to the next, and,
though changeless in content, adapts itself to each generation.
Because of this, the Church is continually in dialogue with society, and each priest is in the forefront of that dialogue, bringing the timeless message of Christ's Gospel to his own day.
Cardinal Ratzinger also emphasizes the authority of the priest-
preacher, one which he shares with the eternal High Priest, and
exercises in His name and by virtue of his sharing in an apostolic succession begun by the Lord Himself.

In his encyclical *Ecclesiam Suam*, Pope Paul VI could not
have been more forceful on the subject of preaching:

> We want to stress once more the very important place
> that preaching still has, especially in the modern Catho-
> lic apostolate and in connection with the dialogue
> which is our present concern. No other form of com-

---

9   *Spiritus Paraclitus*, cited in *Ibid.*, 140.

munication can take its place, not even the exceptionally powerful and effective means provided by modern technology: the press, radio and television. In effect, the apostolate and sacred preaching are more or
less synonymous terms. Preaching is the primary apostolate. Our ministry, Venerable Brethren, is before all
else the ministry of the word.[10]

A decade following the Council, the Holy Father expanded
his theme to include the concept of evangelization. Such is the
grace and vocation proper to the Church, he notes, the Church's
deepest identity. The Church exists to evangelize—to teach and
to preach, to proclaim with authority the word of God. This is
also carried out pastorally and sacramentally, and all three have
as their goal bringing the Gospel message more effectively into
the lives of nations and peoples. In his apostolic exhortation
Evangelii Nuntiandi in 1976, the Pope said that priests are associated with bishops in the ministry of evangelization, a concept
which he defined in broad terms as meaning:

... to proclaim with authority the word of God, to as-
semble the scattered people of God, to feed this people
with the signs of the actions of Christ which are the
sacraments, to set up the people on the road to salvation, to maintain it in that unity in which we are, at
different levels, active and living instruments, and
unceasingly to keep this community gathered around
Christ, faithful to its deepest vocation.[11]

In his Apostolic Constitution on Priestly Formation,
Pastores Dabo Vobis, Pope John Paul II follows closely both Vatican II and Paul VI in his teaching on the priestly ministry of the

---

[10] Cited in Federico Suarez, *About Being a Priest* (Princeton, NJ: Scepter Publishers,
   Inc., 1996), 43-44.
[11] Cited in Avery Dulles, S.J., *The Priestly Office* (New York: Paulist Press, 1997), 23-
   24.

word. In addition, his Encyclical *Redemptoris Missio* expands the theme, teaching that the spiritual gift each priest receives should give him a global view: he must be concerned not merely with the Catholic faithful entrusted to his care, but the much larger human family which has God as its Father:

> At one point in his encyclical John Paul II recalls how Saint Paul journeyed to Athens, the cultural center of the Greco-Roman world, to proclaim the Gospel at the Areopagus, where the most influential intellectuals were accustomed to gather. Today, says the Pope, a new culture is emerging under the aegis of contemporary means of communication. If the Gospel is to make contact with this culture, people of faith must be at home with new languages, new techniques and new psychology. In speaking of new Areopagi, John Paul II adverts to the new worlds of scientific research, economics, political science, and international relations. Ordinarily speaking, he says, it will be the task of the laity to permeate the sciences and professions with Christian values and thus to bridge the gap between faith and culture. But it is the task of priests to motivate these initiatives and to arouse a lively ecclesial consciousness in lay apostles.[12]

The priestly ministry of the word has also its practical side, namely one's preparation and inner dispositions. Regarding the latter, the priest must be specially careful in the matter of faithfulness, for it is Christ's teaching, not his own opinion, that he must make known, and Christ's teaching as it has been handed down through the Church, without any personal interpretations or additions. Centuries ago, Saint Vincent of Lerins addressed this concern, and left no doubt about the preacher's role:

> "Guard what has been entrusted to you" (1 Timothy 6:20). But what is something that has been entrusted

---

[12] *Ibid.*, 26-27.

to you? It is what has been given to you, not what you yourself have found; what you have received, not what you thought up; not a matter of invention but of doctrine; not of private use but of public tradition… whose author your should not be, but its guardian.… Preserve inviolate and spotless the talent of the Catholic faith. What was entrusted to you, you should keep and you should hand over. You have received gold; deliver gold… do not shamefully replace the gold with lead.… Teach the same things as you have learned, though you may say things in a new way, do not say new things.[13]

So much of the solidity of Catholic faith is to be found in the homily at Holy Mass—the one weekly opportunity the priest has to instruct the faithful in faith and morals. The Second Vatican Council, in its Decree on the Sacred Liturgy, *Sacrosanctum Concilium*, reminds us that the Mass is composed of two essential parts: the liturgy of the word and the Eucharistic liturgy, and that these comprise one single act of faith. Within that central mystery, it is the homily, whose inspiration is drawn from the sacred texts appropriate to each liturgical season, that provides the guiding light for each believer's pilgrim journey through this world. It is, therefore, vitally important that a priest prepare exceedingly well, and that he be a man who thinks with the teaching Church at the very core of his being. Orthodox preparation, coupled with a personal love of the Eucharistic Lord will bear fruit beyond all telling; lack of the same will produce a very opposite effect:

> The preacher without the Spirit of Christ is like Giezi whom Elias sent to revive a dead man. Although he brought with him the prophet's staff, no miracle happened, for the virtue of the staff was negated by the hands that held it (4 Kings 4:25-38). One may hold the Scriptures of the Lord in the pulpit, as Giezi held the

---

[13] Cited in Suarez, *op. cit.*, 45-46.

staff in his hand, but no souls are saved. The absence of an inner spiritual life makes sermonizing dull, stale, flat and unprofitable.[14]

These thoughts from the late Archbishop Fulton J. Sheen reflect his belief that no preacher will really be effective without spending time in the presence of the Blessed Sacrament. Sheen prepared many of his own talks before Christ's Eucharistic presence, and strongly encouraged his fellow priests in the same practice. In particular, Eucharistic visits should focus on the following Sunday's homily, and a prayer to the Holy Spirit before delivering it could produce "a Pentecostal fire":

> Every person to whom we preach we shall meet again on the judgment day. How great our joy, then, if we have rectified their consciences and elevated them to the embrace of the Sacred Heart. No wonder that Moses, Elias and Jeremias all tried to run away from the crushing burden of delivering the Word of the Lord.[15]

In his Second Letter to the Corinthians, Saint Paul said, "I believed, and so I spoke" (4:13). That is every preacher's belief; that is every preacher's joy.

---

[14] Fulton J. Sheen, *The Priest Is Not His Own* (New York: McGraw Hill Book Company, Inc., 1963), 126. The Scripture citation is from 2 Kings. The Vulgate 1-4 Kings=1 and 2 Samuel, and 1 and 2 Kings. Giezi=Gehazi. The prophet Elisha (Eliseus) figures in this story, not Elijah (Elias).

[15] *Ibid.*, 128.

9

The Gift of Priestly Celibacy

"Celibacy," writes one theologian, "is one of those signs that
reminds us of Christ's absolute demands, of His liberating return, of the economy of the kingdom of heaven, of the need to
be vigilant, to break with the world, with the flesh, with lust,
and, with the joy in our hearts, to accept renunciation of the
passions for pure love of Jesus."[1] Such an observation leaves no
doubt of the urgent need in our times to maintain this priceless
treasure, this gift given by Jesus Christ, the Eternal High Priest
to all those He has called and configures to Himself in the sacrament of Holy Orders.

Celibacy is, first and foremost, a gift; it is also a discipline
whose origins have been studied very carefully by historians.
Until recently, the prevailing view was that no uniform legislation existed for the first three centuries of the Church's life. In
305 A.D., a local Church Council in Elvira, Spain issued a document calling on bishops and priests to live a celibate life. If a
priest were married, said the Council, he should abstain from
relations with his wife. In the East, the first major Council was
held at Nicea in 325 A.D. It was universal in scope, especially
with its creedal pronouncement, but took no stand on celibacy
except to say that a priest must always avoid giving scandal by

---

[1] Max Thurian, "The Theological Basis for Priestly Celibacy," in *For Love Alone*
(Middlegreen, Slough: ST PAULS Publications, 1993), 54.

having any woman other than his wife in his home. In the late seventh century, a Byzantine council, *In Trullo*, accepted the idea of a married presbyterate. Hence, historians have traced the beginnings of the East-West difference on this subject to the early fourth century, with an even sharper distinction by the seventh. In recent years, other scholars, the Jesuit Christian Cochini among them, have carefully scrutinized the words of the Council of Carthage in 390 A.D., and from one particular passage they begin to build an argument that the roots of ecclesial discipline for a celibate clergy are discernable:

> It is proper that the sacred bishops, the priests of God, as well as deacons, or those who are at the service of the divine sacraments, should be absolutely continent in order to obtain in all simplicity what they ask for from God: so that what the Apostles taught and antiquity itself has observed we might also observe.[2]

Clearly, some of the apostles were married men. The Fathers of the Church differed on who were and who were not; they stressed the unimportance of belaboring the point. What is far more reflective of the early Church's attitude is found in Scripture:

> There is no one who has given up home, or wife, brothers, parents, or children, for the sake of the kingdom of God, who will not be repaid many times over in this age, and in the age to come have eternal life.[3]

Saint Paul had a particularly strong influence on such early Christian writers as John Chrysostom and Clement of Alexandria:

---

[2] Cited from the *Codex Canonum Ecclesiae Africanae* of 419 in P.P. Joannov, *Discipline Generale Antique* (Ile-Txe Sibelle), 1.2. in Aidan Nichols, O.P., *Holy Order* (Dublin: Veritas, 1990), 156.

[3] Luke 18:28-30.

I want you to be free from anxious care. The unmarried man cares for the Lord's business; his aim is to please the Lord. But the married man cares for worldly things; his aim is to please his wife; and he has a divided mind. The unmarried or celibate woman cares for the Lord's business; her aim is to be dedicated to Him in body as in spirit; but the married woman cares for worldly things; her aim is to please her husband. In saying this I have no wish to keep you on a tight rein. I am thinking simply of your own good, of what is seemly, and of your freedom to wait upon the Lord without distraction.[4]

They argued that if the Corinthian laity were so strongly encouraged to abstain from marital relations at certain intervals to more completely give themselves to the Lord, how much more important was such an admonition for those in the celibate state. Even the Byzantine council, *In Trullo*, which had been convened by Emperor Justinian II in 691-692, stresses the importance of sexual abstinence when priests are preparing to offer the Eucharistic mysteries.

While the history of the discipline of celibacy may have been debated on particular points, the theology and spirituality underlying it is enormously rich. The reasons, of course, are Christological. Celibacy always has, and always will have, great relevance because Our Lord Jesus Christ will always have great relevance. He lived His earthly life at a time when society looked askance at those leaving no progeny in the world, yet He clearly chose to combine His role as Priest, Prophet and King with the celibate state. His relationship with the Church He founded is a spousal one, and the extent of His spousal commitment was His willingness to die for His bride. Every man who shares Christ's priesthood is called to have that same degree of commitment, that same spousal love for Christ's Mystical Body:

---

[4] 1 Corinthians 7:32-35.

The priest is the living image of Jesus Christ, the Spouse of the Church. But Christ is Spouse in a special way in the sacrifice of Calvary, because the Church as Bride "proceeds like a new Eve from the open side of the Redeemer on the Cross." Christ's supreme priestly act is then a spousal one, as Saint Paul explains when he encourages husbands and wives to love each other "as Christ loved the Church and gave Himself up for her" (Ephesians 5:25). This is why "Christ stands 'before' the Church, and 'nourishes and cherishes her'" (5:29), giving His life for her.[5]

It is, therefore, in the Eucharistic sacrifice that every man who has assented to follow Christ in the priesthood, and strictly adhere to His way of life truly lives out this spousal relationship. The reason why every priest can do this so effectively is because of the change in his very being which occurred at the moment he received the sacrament of Holy Orders. In philosophical language it is called an ontological change and, by its very uniqueness, it is seen as a basis for celibacy:

The appropriateness of celibacy may be grasped more precisely by grounding it on the priestly character. Character means consecration and conformity to Christ the Shepherd. When consecration reaches the depth of personal being, it calls for an expression of itself in the way the person lives, or at least in the general orientation of one's life. True, consecration does not include absolute determinations in this respect, nor does it, as such, impose precise and detailed obligations, but it does seek to concretize itself by letting God exercise an ever more total dominance over the self. Celibacy is the best of these concretizations. By requiring that life be celibate, consecration gains control over one's heart, and activity. Conformity, too, is more complete when

---

[5] Thomas J. McGovern, *Priestly Identity: A Study in the Theology of the Priesthood* (Dublin: Four Courts Press, Ltd., 2001), 113.

it entails a sharing in the way of life by which Christ discharged His mission as shepherd with a more universal love.[6]

George Basil Hume, late Cardinal Archbishop of Westminster, England, describes it in more practical terms:

> If I had no arguments in favor of celibacy, I would look no further than the person of the Lord, and He was celibate. I would find that totally satisfying. I would say to myself: I do not understand, I cannot answer any questions, it is enough for me that He was celibate. Why He was, and why it was so important, I will only know later on.[7]

The Cardinal went on to point out that far from stifling the heart or killing love, celibacy channels a priest's affections to feed and enrich his pastoral concern and care for those whom he is sent to serve. This becomes clearer if it is understood biblically, especially in the two creation narratives one finds in the book of Genesis:

> In the second account, the importance of companionship and mutual support is underlined: "It is not good that the man should be alone; I will make him a helper" (Genesis 2:18). The first creation narrative, on the other hand, emphasizes the importance of that God-given instinct whereby two persons in becoming one flesh "increase and multiply" (Genesis 1:28). These two accounts show human love as unitive and procreative. Love between man and woman is God-given, God-inspired, and therefore good. When we reflect on celibacy, such thoughts as these are the starting point. Celibacy is an extraordinary gift, a spiritual charism,

---

[6] Jean Galot, S.J., *Theology of the Priesthood* (San Francisco: Ignatius Press, 1985), 244.
[7] Basil Hume, O.S.B., *Light in the Lord* (Middlegreen, Slough: ST PAULS Publications, 1991), 36.

and one we must learn to treasure in humility and in prayer. It is not the natural inclination of normal humanity but a special commitment for one's own sake but even more for others. There is no protection for celibacy outside of prayer and a proper understanding of what it means to be creatively celibate.[8]

Spiritual writers maintain there are strong pastoral reasons for the celibate life, especially in the twenty-first century. We live in times when the concept of a lifetime commitment is not always taken seriously. The late Archbishop Fulton J. Sheen, in his retreat conferences to priests, often referred to marriages not lived out until death do them part, and chalices left in sacristies. The logical conclusion would seem to follow that a pastoral sensitivity needed in today's Church is one which understands the human condition, within the larger context of the transformation of society according to the Gospel ethic and the challenge it extends to all believers, but especially priests. The radicalism of life embraced by Christ, counter cultural as it surely was, must find its twenty-first century counterpart in the life of every priest. Marriage, taken as an equally demanding and sacrificial lifetime commitment, would legitimately make demands on any man, which would greatly hinder a life of total consecration to the Lord and His Church.

Celibacy has deep eschatological roots as well; it is a life pointing to heaven, a life which serves as a continuous reminder to all on their earthly pilgrimage, of the transitory nature of this life, of how quickly an earthly existence passes, and of the unending reality for which all of us were made. It points to a world where marriage, procreation and the passing of generations will no longer be the norm. It is a reminder not to become too attached to the things of this world; each generation which has enjoyed them has had to part with them when their earthly sojourn has been completed. Our Lord referred to this very point

---

[8] *Ibid.*, 34.

when, in response to a rather sarcastic question put to Him by the Pharisees about the woman married seven times, and whose she would be in the next world, He responded:

> The men and women of this world marry; but those who have been judged worthy of a place in the other world and of the resurrection from the dead, do not marry, for they are not subject to death any longer. They are like angels; they are sons of God, because they share in the resurrection.[9]

Since, by Our Lord's own admission, marrying and being given in marriage will not be part of the Kingdom of God, the point has been made that marriage has its roots in the old order of creation, whereas the origins of celibacy are traceable to the new order of the Gospel. The fullness of love to be experienced in the heavenly reign finds only a weak reflection in the deepest intimacies of earthly, human love. Priests, then, are reflections of that love which knows no bounds, and is being prepared by the Lord for all who have loved Him faithfully:

> Since Christ was unmarried, we may find it strange at first that the Council speaks of fatherhood in Christ. Yet the hymn *Summi Parentis Filio* speaks of Christ as father of the world to come. If we bear in mind what Saint Paul teaches us about the spousal love of Christ for His Church, we will see that this "world to come" is nothing less than the child of that union, the fruit of that love…. It is not for nothing that the priest is addressed as "Father" by his people. As with the fatherhood of Christ, that of the priest points to the world to come; his solitude and earthly barrenness, a prefiguring of death; his prayer, pastoral charity and spiritual fruitfulness, a sign of God's power which is at work now to sanctify and so to yield eternal life.[10]

---

[9] Luke 20:34-36.

[10] J. Francis Cardinal Stafford, "The Mystery of the Priestly Vocation," *Origins* 18.22 (10 November 1988), cited in Nichols, *op. cit.*, 163-164.

In its Decree on Priestly Life and Ministry, *Presbyterorum Ordinis*, the Second Vatican Council stressed that celibacy enables a priest better to actualize his consecration to Christ with undivided love. It allows him much more freedom in his striving to be all things to all people. It gives him a universal sort of openness, permits him to totally expend the creative energies of his mind and heart, and allows him to take on a spiritual fatherhood whose dimensions are incredibly far-reaching. This spiritual fatherhood has very practical components in every priest's life:

> Celibacy has a deep inner affinity with the calling to be a priest and, consequently, it is misleading to speak of the "burden of celibacy" as if priesthood and celibacy were in some sense irreconcilable. The priest who lives for Christ and from Christ usually has no insurmountable difficulties in living out this charism. He is not immune to the normal temptations of the flesh but, as a result of his ascetical training, the daily cultivation of his spiritual life, and the distancing of himself from anything which could constitute a danger to his chastity, he will encounter joy in his vocation and experience a deep spiritual paternity in bringing supernatural life to souls.[11]

Some years after the Council's conclusion, Pope Paul VI wrote a letter on clerical celibacy, *Sacerdotalis Caelibatus*, in which he draws on the rich tradition of the Church to make the connection between the celibacy of Christ and His redemptive work. In addition, the Holy Father considers influences beyond the kind operative in the early Church which, nonetheless, influenced Christian thought. The most notable among these would be the ideal of ritual continence in the pagan cults of Greece and Rome, the rejection of sexual pleasure in Stoic phi-

---

[11] McGovern, *op. cit.*, 115.

losophy and even the deprecation of the body one finds in such philosophies as neo-Platonism. In so doing, though, the Pope refuses to speak of ministerial celibacy without, in the same breath, celebrating the transfiguration of marriage by the grace of Christ:

> Marriage, which, by God's will, continues the work of the first creation, taken up into the total design of salvation, also acquires (with the Redemption) a new meaning and value. Jesus, in fact, has re-established its primordial dignity, honored it and raised it to the dignity of a sacrament and mysterious sign of His union with the Church.... But Christ as Mediator of a yet more excellent Covenant, opened, too, a new way in which the human creature, adhering totally and directly to the Lord, and preoccupied solely with Him and His affairs, manifests in a clearer and more complete manner the profoundly innovative reality of the New Testament.[12]

The further we go into the twenty-first century, the greater relevance such words take on—at least in the minds of believers. It is also true that the gap between faith and unbelief in modern culture appears to widen: for all those who become convinced of the relationship between holiness of life and consecrated celibacy, the secular world provides a corresponding disbelief. Joachim Cardinal Meisner, Archbishop of Cologne, captures the spirit of the secular mind as he explains the only true basis for celibacy:

> For a person who does not experience the existence of Jesus Christ, for a person who does not believe in Him, the celibate is, in fact, a madman or somebody who is sick. Consequently they do not even conceive or tolerate that others can live it. It is not a problem related to

---

[12] *Acta Apostolicae Sedis* 59 (1967), 657-697, cited in Nichols, *op. cit.*, 161.

canon law or to dogma, but to faith in God; a man can come so close to God that he prefers union with God to any other type of union. Celibacy cannot be explained by sociological, psychological or pedagogical reasons, but only by spiritual and theological ones. Without prayer, without dialogue with God, celibacy makes no sense. I repeat: if a person does not take God seriously, he will not be able to understand the essence of celibacy.[13]

The German Cardinal saw an interesting parallel between the gift of celibacy and the story of Our Lord's going to Bethany, and Mary anointing His feet with very expensive perfume. Such an act of love provoked the sarcasm of Judas, who complained that the money wasted on such an act might have better been given to the poor. This reaction is like the mean-spiritedness one finds in the worldly response to celibacy as an unexplainable absurdity. Meisner asks if it is not true that the Lord "merits" that men would give their lives totally to Him. What the world fails to understand is not why so many men have answered the Lord's invitation, but why they are called in the first place. It is nothing less than love responding to Love, but surely not a love which secularity easily comprehends. The fact is, celibacy will continue to exist in Christ's Church since His magnanimity will never cease, and the human heart will always respond. Christ would never deprive His Church of that which has enriched it for so many centuries, for such would constitute real impoverishment. For the Church's part, she will continue to be faithful to her Lord, and one of the most splendid ways that faithfulness manifests itself is in the lives of those who give themselves totally and without reserve to Him.

Perhaps one of the strongest appeals to the heart in defense of celibacy in modern times has come from Mother Teresa of Calcutta, in an address in which she likened celibacy to a sign

---

[13] *Osservatore Romano*, 25 October 1992, cited in McGovern, *op. cit.*, 120-121.

of the charity of Christ. Mother Teresa's approach was not scholarly—it didn't have to be. Mother made the point that just as God our Father prepared a worthy dwelling place for His Son in the immaculate womb of a virgin, so it is fitting that a priest prepares himself to take the place of Jesus, the Son of God, by freely choosing priestly celibacy. The gift of this lifestyle, she notes, prepares both the priest and those he serves for eternal life, since Jesus calls each of His priests to be His co-workers, filling heaven with His children:

> Your priestly celibacy is the terrible emptiness you experience. God cannot fill what is full, He can only fill emptiness—deep poverty, and your *yes* is the beginning of being or becoming empty. It is not how much we really "have" to give, but how empty we are—so that we can receive fully in our life and let Him live His life in us. Priestly celibacy is not just not getting married, not to have a family. It is undivided love of Christ in chastity. Nothing and nobody will separate me from the love of Christ. It is not simply a list of don'ts; it is love. Freedom to love and to be all things to all people. And for that we need the freedom of poverty and simplicity of life. Jesus could have everything but He chose to have nothing. We too must choose not to have or to use certain luxuries.[14]

Mother went on to explain that for her, the priesthood is the sacredness, the holiness for which Christ has come to earth to become man, to live His Father's love and compassion, and to wash away sin. The priest is the connecting link between humanity and God, the one called to proclaim Christ, His saving instrument, a man who had given God permission to do with him exactly as He wills:

---

[14] Mother Teresa of Calcutta, "Priestly Celibacy: Sign of the Charity of Christ," in *For Love Alone, op. cit.*, 211-213.

Yes, the world is in need of priests, of holy priests, of priestly celibacy, for the world is in need of Christ. To doubt the value of one's priesthood and one's priestly celibacy in today's world is to doubt the very value of Christ and His mission—for they are one. Christ's mission is ours.[15]

---

[15] *Ibid.*, 217.

10

Priesthood in the Third Millennium

A contemporary writer on the priesthood has offered this description of Sacred Orders for the third millennium:

> We are Christ the Head made visible in this place and time for the purpose of drawing humankind to community with Christ to the glory of the Father in union with the Holy Spirit. This is the ontological aspect that makes our priesthood different from the priesthood of all the faithful. As Vatican Council II stated, it is a difference in kind, not just degree.[1]

Nothing novel, perhaps, but much in need of restating in a post-conciliar Church which has seen much emphasis on the role of the laity, especially in the Church's sacramental life. The author went on to describe the one priesthood of Jesus Christ, the sole mediator between God and man. All the baptized share in the priesthood in varying degrees, be it in the priesthood of the faithful or the ministerial priesthood. The latter is very unique and different from the former in that a sacramental unity exists between bishops, who possess the fullness of the priesthood, and priests and deacons who are their collaborators. The Church

---

[1] M. Basil Pennington, O.S.C.O. and Carl J. Arico, *Living Our Priesthood Today* (Huntington, IN: Our Sunday Visitor, Inc., 1987), 34.

is the Mystical Body of Christ—that instrument through which the Lord draws all into communion with Himself and one another, and Christ Himself is a sacrament—God made present in a Divine Person with two natures, human and divine. The ministerial priesthood corresponds to the sacrament of Christ the Head; the priesthood of the faithful, to Christ the members. It is very true that those who belong to the ministerial priesthood are also part of the believing faithful, while the laity share by collaboration in the hierarchical priesthood. It is also true that the difference between both priesthoods is clear, distinct, and very easily definable.

This unambiguous, ontological change in a man's being elicits the same vocational commitment from the man of the twenty-first century as in any other period of history. One bishop, reminding his clergy they were not functionaries, but "bridges to the mystery of God," noted that any priest who so defined himself would really discover his true meaning. It was strongly reminiscent of the Cure of Ars' observation that if a priest were truly conscious of who he was and the power that was really his, he probably would die.

Giving a retreat to priests at Ars in 1986, Pope John Paul II expressed concern about any modern description which identified a priest solely within the context of his functions. In stressing the modern priest's very real configuration to Christ, the Holy Father was responding to certain contemporary thinkers and writers who have maintained that mystery is no longer present in the priesthood. In fact, he was saying the mystery is, and always will be, present in each individual priest, a mystery captured well by Cardinal John Henry Newman:

> We approach and, in spite of the darkness, our hands or our head or our brow or our lips become, as it were, sensible of the contact of something more than earthly. We know not where we are, but we have been bathing in water, and a voice tells us it is blood. Or we have a mark signed upon our foreheads, and it spoke of

Calvary. Or we recollect a hand laid upon our heads, and surely it had the print of nails on it, and resembled His who with a touch gave sight to the blind and raised the dead. Or we have been eating and drinking, and it was not a dream surely, that one fed us from His wounded side, and renewed our nature by the heavenly food He gave.[2]

It is a mystery always present, and there appears to be a growing awareness in today's laity of what they expect of priests. If the expectation is demanding, it is so only because of Christ's priesthood in which men are invited to share. It has caused one contemporary writer to focus on his own priesthood:

I stand in awe of the interior journey that I am being called to. I stand in awe of the depths of the love within the people that I journey with, in awe of their love for me as a man, Christian and priest. I stand in awe of the Church in the profoundness of its Christ-presence in the world—the Church, with all its strengths and weaknesses, still being a presence of Christ in this world here and now.[3]

People would only have such regard for one who truly had made the priesthood his own, one who was clearly marked as another Christ. The process does not begin on ordination day— that is the culmination of several years of prayer, study, and discernment. A seminary rector reminded those young men under his charge that when a man says yes to the priesthood, that yes is forever. He was speaking of priestly fidelity and echoing Mother Teresa's observation of some years ago, that the Lord is not calling His priests to success; He is calling them to faithfulness. Fidelity is easy when one's priestly life is happy, the

---

[2] Cited in Timothy M. Dolan, *Priests for the Third Millennium* (Huntington, IN: Our Sunday Visitor, Inc., 2000), 272-273.

[3] Pennington, *op. cit.*, 20.

rector reminded his students, but what happens when the inevitable sorrow, loneliness and frustration set in? Is it still possible to remain faithful? It is, he pointed out, if our faithfulness is not to a position, but to an identity, a knowledge that we are other Christs—changed men. He also used terms like doubt, fatigue, dryness, anger, frustration and confusion, telling his seminarians that such were to be expected in the living out of one's priestly existence, but not to be seen negatively. It was in each of these circumstances that a priest's fidelity is really proven.

Writing to priests some years earlier, Basil Cardinal Hume made the point even more concrete when he equated fidelity with learning to embrace the cross as it is laid on a man's priestly shoulders:

> I am not thinking of anything particularly dramatic. I am thinking of all the frustrations and disappointments of everyday life, the anger we can experience when we feel ignored and unappreciated or the appointment to a parish which seems to you totally unsuited to you.[4]

Fidelity, then, is at the core of the priest's being; there is no day off, no time away from it, no accepting it at certain times but not others. The reason is quite simple: the priesthood is not something external, an occupational way of life we are associated with. It is an internal identity, totally captivating one's being. In a pastoral letter to the priests of the Archdiocese of New York, the late John Cardinal O'Connor captured these precise statements:

> I have no memory quite like that of lying flat on my face on the cold stone of the sanctuary of Sts. Peter and Paul Cathedral in Philadelphia on the day of my ordination. Some of you have heard me evoke that moment

---

[4] Basil Hume, O.S.B., *Light in the Lord* (Middlegreen, Slough: ST PAULS Publications, 1991), 129.

when I ordain the priests of New York in Saint Patrick's Cathedral or elsewhere. For me that is the moment of total consecration on the part of the ordained, complete surrender, Christ on the Cross. Every time I ordain, my hope is the same: that when each newly ordained priest rises from the floor, as Peter and James and John on the Mount of the Transfiguration, he will look up and see only Jesus for the rest of his life, everywhere, in everyone, including himself. As Cardinal Suhard puts it, the newly ordained is himself "transfigured" with Christ as Christ. In the act of prostration, the priest dies to himself for the world. It is fitting that during the prostration we call upon all the saints of all the centuries, the continuity of our faith.[5]

This is the priestly identity which finds fullest expression in our priestly fidelity. A poem attributed to Saint Norbert puts it another way:

O priest, who are you?
Not through yourself, for you are drawn from nothing.
Not for yourself, since you are the mediator of humanity.
Not to yourself, for you are married to the Church.
Not to your own, for you are the servant of all.
You are not you, for you are God.
Who are you, then?
You are nothing, and everything.[6]

Priestly identity in the third millennium allows for no ambiguity—neither does the priest himself, and the sort of man he is expected to be at this moment in the Church's life. Essentially, he is to be what he always was—another Christ. Archbishop Timothy M. Dolan of Milwaukee was a former rector of the North American College in Rome. In a series of conferences

---

[5] John Cardinal O'Connor, *Always a Priest, Always Present* (New York: Archdiocese of New York, 1989), 47.
[6] Cited in Dolan, *op. cit.*, 238.

given to Roman seminarians, he concentrated on two major thematic areas for priests today: living the Christian life, and living the priestly life. In discussing the first, Dolan focused on the theological virtues of faith, hope and charity, showing how each applied to the priest in today's Church. He then considered humility, fidelity, obedience, courtesy, integrity, prudence, a frequent use of the sacrament of Penance in the life of a seminarian and a priest, human formation, stewardship of spirit, patience, simplicity of life and joy. Hardly new themes—in fact, valid topics for priests' retreats in almost any generation. The point the Archbishop was trying to make was the timeless nature of these formative issues in their preparatory years before ordination, and also areas of concern to which priests in every generation have to give serious attention.

For the priest, living the Christian life and living the priestly life each flow from the universal call to holiness incumbent on all the Lord's followers. For the laity, their baptism into Christ's life is the basic mandate for their constant striving for spiritual perfection; for the priest his baptismal commitment has been shaped in a unique way by his reception of the sacrament of Holy Orders. This sacrament gives a specific orientation to the gift given him at Baptism, and although he has been doubly configured to Christ, the Vatican Council emphasized that the priest has only one vocation to holiness; the graces to carry out that vocation have to be enormous.

Within that call to holiness, the lay person may well find a close affinity with the hidden life of Our Lord at Nazareth, since everything about it gives value and profound meaning to all the particulars of daily life and work. For the priest, Our Lord's public life of preaching and teaching will be more the point of reference, since his own priestly life so closely resembles that of the Master. Approaches to priestly spirituality have varied with writers through the generations, but all come back to one central idea: Christ and His priesthood. Only there will each priest find the core of his spiritual grounding; more specifically:

The concept of following Christ brings us back to the community formed by the disciples who accompanied Jesus along the roads of Judea and Galilee, listening to His teaching and sharing His life. From the pages of the New Testament we see that to follow Christ is to share in His sentiments (cf. Philippians 2:5), to have the same availability to do the will of the Father (cf. John 4:34), and to be ready to give one's life for the love of the brethren (cf. John 5:12-13).[7]

The following of Christ and a priest's prayer life are synonymous. His prayer life has much to do with his insertion into the sacramental life of the Church—not simply his administration of the sacraments to others, but his own deep relationship with the Eucharist, his own frequenting of the sacrament of Penance, etc. In addition to the sacraments, the Liturgy of the Hours, or official prayer of the Church is stressed over and again by writers on the contemporary priesthood. It is time, say many, that priests come back to an appreciation of the tremendous richness to be found in the prayer still very much mandated by Holy Mother Church for all priests. Father Basil Pennington, in his work, *Living Our Priesthood Today*, has made the point that all priests need sacred study, that is, reading geared to the intellect, to knowing and understanding revelation and all that revelation teaches us. There is a deep faith in every priest, one which is constantly seeking understanding; a faith which needs to be enlightened so that it might be properly explained to people of each generation; an immutable teaching made relevant today, much like Cardinal Newman's development of doctrine. This is why sacred study is so important to the priest.

In addition to study for the development of his mind, Pennington also makes the point that a priest needs another type of reading for the strengthening of his will. The commitment he made on his ordination day needs to be renewed every day

---

[7]   Thomas J. McGovern, *Priestly Identity: a Study in the Theology of Priesthood* (Dublin: Four Courts Press, 2002), 126.

of his priestly life; such can only be accomplished by the sort of reading that gives new insights to timeless ideas, new approaches that will rekindle the flame of love which is always to be kept burning. Finally, there is a third type of reading, geared neither to the mind nor will exclusively, but one which allows for a man's personal encounter with God, the sort of approach which seeks to go beyond mere words to the very personal experience of God in the priestly life. Pennington feels all three needs are well met in the Liturgy of the Hours. It would be rare that a priest would feel the presence of all three needs fulfilled every time he recites the Divine Office; rather, one need will be more satisfied at one time, one at another. Though the Office has many components, the Psalms, those most ancient of prayers, have particular relevance for the priest. In them he will find all human emotions described, and the working out of those emotions in his own spiritual life. Centuries ago, Saint Ambrose went even further than the emotional level, writing that, although all Scripture is filled with God's grace for our lives, in the Psalms the entire paschal mystery of Our Lord could be discovered. The Hours are, therefore, an invitation on the part of Christ to every priest, and for that matter, to all the baptized, to enter into a very special relationship with Him. The Code of Canon Law puts it aptly:

> ... the Church, fulfilling the priestly function of Christ, celebrates the Liturgy of the Hours, whereby hearing God speaking to His people and memorializing the mystery of salvation, the Church praises Him without interruption and intercedes for the salvation of the whole world.[8]

Each priest, at his deaconate ordination, is asked if he is resolved to celebrate faithfully the Liturgy of the Hours for the Church and the whole world. By his acceptance, he joins his

---

[8]   *Code of Canon Law* (Washington, DC: Canon Law Society of America, 1983), #1173, 425.

brothers in the priestly fraternity throughout the entire world in praying with and for the Church. Such prayer is absolutely essential for the Church's welfare, and for the preservation of the priest's vocation. That is why the daily recitation of the Office is a *sine qua non* of the priestly existence. The General Instruction on the Liturgy of the Hours leaves no doubt about the obligation of those in Sacred Orders:

> Bishops and priests, therefore, and other sacred ministers who have received from the Church the mandate to celebrate the Liturgy of the Hours, are to recite the whole sequence of hours each day, preserving as far as possible the genuine relationship of the hours to the time of day. They are to give due importance to the hours which are the two hinges on which this Liturgy turns, that is, Lauds as morning prayer and Vespers: let them take care not to omit these hours, unless for a serious reason. They are also to carry out faithfully the Office of the Readings, which is above all the liturgical celebration of the word of God. Thus, they will carry out daily that duty of welcoming into themselves the word of God. That the day may be completely sanctified, they will desire to recite the middle hour and compline, thus commending themselves to God and completing the entire "Opus Dei" before going to bed.[9]

One spiritual writer has compared the priest reciting his Office to dropping in on a conversation already in progress, one that began long before he was born, and will go on long after he has left this earth. The description very poignantly unites the priest with the entire Communion of Saints, triumphant in heaven and suffering anticipated love in Purgatory. It allows one to feel the presence of Our Lady, the Angels, the Saints, the long priestly fellowship which has preceded him in this world, and even his

---

[9] Cited in Dolan, *op. cit.*, 258.

own forebears in the faith, all united in continuous prayer to the heavenly Father. The prayer recommended to priests before the recitation of the Office says it all:

> Lord God, I offer this Divine Office to you, together with the adoration and praise of the angels and saints in heaven, as well as that of all the priests of your Church and all other consecrated souls. I present to you, heavenly Father, through the Immaculate Heart of Mary, this chorus of prayer, made holy in the Sacred Heart of Jesus and made one with His most holy prayer. May all the words of this prayer be acts of pure love, adoration, thanksgiving, satisfaction, trust and surrender to Your holy will. Let this prayer be for my weak self a spiritual communion, an act of humility, and of perfect self-denial: and may it be a sacrifice of praise and glory to you, O Blessed Trinity. Amen.[10]

The third millennium is apt to find priests engaged in such apostolates as health care, education, prison work, the classroom, the military, and most particularly, the parish. Apropos of the parish is the oft told story of a group of priests received in audience by Blessed John XXIII; one a chancellor, one a university president, a college professor, a hospital chaplain, and a parish priest. Each was told to introduce himself and tell the Holy Father his title. The parish priest felt a bit intimidated among the others, but when he introduced himself as a parish priest, the Pope genuflected to him and said "that is the most important work of all." Regardless of whether a priest finds himself on the front lines of parish duty, or in one of the specialized works, he is in constant pursuit of holiness. John Cardinal O'Connor saw all spiritual growth epitomized by the gifts of the Holy Spirit to the priest, and two in particular were a spirit of poverty, and a fruitful use of virginity.

---

[10] *Ibid.*, 266.

O'Connor reminded his priests that the spirit of poverty is what was once referred to as detachment. While the diocesan priest does not take the formal vow of poverty, he must look carefully at his use of and desire for material possessions, always maintaining a balance between their legitimate use and misuse. At the same time, the priest must ask himself if he views his virginity as negative and unproductive. Every celibate can give spiritual birth to countless souls if he gives himself to Christ with the same passion a man and woman give themselves to one another. Such is becoming a celibate for the sake of the Kingdom, and is directly related to priestly vocations:

> All love seeks to reproduce itself. I know that you love your priesthood as I love mine. If we were married men, we would want to reproduce our love by way of children. We are celibates, but we love. Our love for the priesthood can and should encourage others to become priests. We must really want this. Why shouldn't we? I have spoken... of the suffering inherent in the priesthood, the loneliness, the sacrifice. I see in this, however, no contradiction with what is for me the sheer joy of being a priest.[11]

Such are some of the themes emerging from the literature on the priesthood in the third millennium. One finds a great stress laid on strengthening priestly spirituality, and thereby strengthening priestly identity. At least one author, underscoring this point, has related the story of Saint Maximilian Kolbe, the Polish Franciscan who offered his life in the concentration camp of Auschwitz so that a married man and father might go free. When asked his identity, Kolbe did not reply with his nationality, nor that he was a friend, nor even the generic answer that he shared a common humanity with the prisoner to be executed; rather, he responded that he was a Catholic priest. Such horrific

---

[11] O'Connor, *op. cit.*, 42.

conditions as found at Auschwitz could not, for one moment, erase that basic identity from Father Kolbe's mind. That same sense of a strong, personal priestly identity is surely at the heart of the Church today, and was certainly in the mind of John Cardinal O'Connor as he wrote these words to the priests of New York:

> It's always a stunning thing for me to realize that Christ called each of us by name, out of all the hundreds of millions of people who ever lived. And that He called each of us, His priests, to be His companions, His friends in a unique way. Yet I believe it to be exceedingly important that we be convinced of this reality: No matter who else rejects us, Christ really wants us to be His friends. "You have not chosen me but I have chosen you" (John 15:16). One of the most poignant moments in Christ's life, it seems to me, came when "many turned from Him and walked with Him no more," so that He asked His chosen Apostles: "Will you, too, turn away?" (John 6:66-67). He needs us....[12]

---

[12] *Ibid.*, 47.

11

The Priestly Theology of John Paul II

Since his election to the papacy in 1978, our Holy Father, Pope John Paul II, has written extensively on the priesthood, and by personal example, has affected the thinking of many in the Church on the purpose and nature of Holy Orders. In his mind there is no ambiguity:

> What does it mean to be a priest? According to Saint Paul, it means above all to be a steward of the mysteries of God: "This is how one should regard us, as servants of Christ and stewards of the mysteries of God. Now it is required of stewards that they be found trustworthy" (1 Corinthians 4:1-2). The word "steward" cannot be replaced by any other. It is deeply rooted in the Gospel: it brings to mind the parable of the faithful steward and the unfaithful one (Luke 12:41-48). The steward is not the owner, but the one to whom the owner entrusts his goods so that he will manage them justly and responsibly. In exactly the same way, the priest received from Christ the treasures of salvation, in order duly to distribute them among the people among whom he is sent. These treasures are those of faith. The priest is thus a man of the word of God, a man of sacrament, a man of the "mystery of faith." Through faith he draws near to the invisible treasures which constitute the inheritance of the world's re-

demption by the Son of God. No one may consider himself the "owner of these treasures"; they are meant for us all. But, by reason of what Christ laid down, the priest has the task of administering them.[1]

The world situation at the inception of his papacy was anything but conducive to priestly vocations. A materialism manifested in the frantic pursuit of success and pleasure; a rationalistic strain of thought which called into question, and in many instances denied, the supernatural; a spirit of individualism which no longer viewed lifetime commitments as necessary, all contributed in the minds of papal biographers, to a cultural shift which deeply affected the Church. The Holy Father himself was quick to single out the European continent and lament its ever-growing cultural relativism and moral decline. Still, he never abandoned his conviction that solutions were to be found within Christ's mystical body.

In every way, John Paul is a man of the Second Vatican Council, and in his priestly writings this is especially true. Early on, he became convinced that the solution to the confusion which had crept into the thinking of many on the nature of the priesthood was to be found in the Council's teaching. In addition, he has contributed enormously in his own writings which include scores of addresses, Holy Thursday letters to priests throughout the world, reflections on his own golden jubilee of sacerdotal ordination, and, most significantly, a 1992 Apostolic Exhortation, *Pastores Dabo Vobis*. When taken in their entirety, the Pope's meditations respond to two fundamental questions: What is the priesthood? and What does it mean to be a priest today?

As to the priesthood, the Holy Father lays great stress on priestly configuration to Christ the High Priest. He states very clearly that men are ontologically changed, and given an indelible character in Holy Orders. In *Pastores Dabo Vobis*, he further

---

[1] Pope John Paul II, *Gift and Mystery* (New York: Doubleday, 1996), 71-72.

develops this idea, when he writes that the spiritual life of a priest is marked, molded and characterized by the way of thinking and acting proper to Christ, the Head and Shepherd of the Church. Our Lord is Head of the Church, which is His body, and He is Head in a new and unique sense of being a servant, one who "emptied Himself, taking the form of a slave, being born in the likeness of men" (Philippians 2:7-8). The spiritual existence of every priest received its life and inspiration from this type of authority, this sort of service to the Church. Our Holy Father quotes Saint Augustine's admonition to a bishop on the day of his Episcopal ordination:

> He who is head of the people must in the first place realize that he is to be the servant of many. And he should not disdain being such; I say it once again, he should not disdain being the servant of many, because the Lord of lords did not disdain to make Himself our servant.[2]

John Paul notes that Christ presents Himself as the Good Shepherd (John 10:11, 14), not only of Israel, but of all humanity (John 10:16). His entire public life is a manifestation of His pastoral charity; He felt compassion for the crowds because they were like sheep without a shepherd (Matthew 18:9, 35-36); He goes in search of those sheep who stray and become scattered (Matthew 18:12-14), and very joyfully celebrates their return. He gathers and protects them, and is able to call each of them by name (John 10:3). Each priest is, therefore, configured to Christ the Head and Shepherd, and to all that these terms imply. It is a special configuration which sets each priest apart from other believers:

> Of course he will always remain a member of the community as a believer alongside his other brothers and

---

2   Pope John Paul II, *I Will Give You Shepherds* (Boston: Pauline Books & Media, 1992), 41-42.

sisters who have been called by the Spirit, but in virtue of his configuration to Christ the Head and Shepherd, the priest stands in this spousal relationship with regard to the community. Inasmuch as he represents Christ the Head, Shepherd and Spouse of the Church, the priest is placed not only in the Church, but also in the forefront of the Church.[3]

Finally, the internal principle animating and guiding the spiritual life of the priest, because of this unique configuration to Christ the Head and Shepherd, is pastoral charity. This is a gift to each priest from the Holy Spirit, enabling him to give the total gift of himself to the Church, no divided allegiances, no hyphenated giving. Instead, each priest follows the Master who "loved the Church and gave Himself up for her" (Ephesians 5:25).

From this configuration, much follows. For our Holy Father, it is the love of the Eucharist that must be an essential component of every priestly existence. The Pope describes the Holy Sacrifice of the Mass as the "heart and center of the Christian world," and once reminded seminarians that each time a priest offers this central mystery of our faith, his life becomes inserted "into the mystery of the living God." Whenever he does so, the priest is privileged to offer nothing less that the Son offering Himself to His heavenly Father for humanity and for all creation:

> The priesthood, in its deepest reality, is the priesthood of Christ. It is Christ who offers Himself, His body and blood in sacrifice to God the Father, and by this sacrifice makes righteous in the Father's eyes all mankind and indirectly, all creation. The priest, in his daily celebration of the Eucharist, goes to the very heart of this mystery. For this reason the celebration of the

---

[3] *Ibid.*, 43.

Eucharist must be the most important moment of the priest's day, the center of his life.[4]

Our Holy Father speaks at length about the words of consecration, and reflects on his own decades of pronouncing them. He asks what sort of memorial is being recalled as the priest stands at the altar and repeats the words of Our Lord at the Last Supper. He answers just as quickly that it is a memorial in the biblical sense, one which makes present the event itself. It is memory and presence, and the secret of this miracle is the action of the Holy Spirit whom the priest invokes when he extends his hands over the gifts of bread and wine:

> ...thus it is not merely the priest who recalls the events of Christ's passion, death and resurrection; it is also the Holy Spirit who enables this event to be made present on the altar through the ministry of the priest. The priest truly acts *in persona Christi*. What Christ accomplished on the altar of the cross, and what earlier still He has instituted as a sacrament in the Upper Room, the priest now renews by the power of the Holy Spirit. At this moment the priest is as it were embraced by the power of the Holy Spirit and the words which he utters have the same efficacy as those spoken by Christ at the Last Supper.[5]

John Paul's writings seem continually to emphasize the priest's need to give thanks for the great privilege which is his, and to savor the mystery. On the occasion of the great jubilee of the year 2000, he traveled to the Holy Land, visited the Cenacle or Upper Room, and from there addressed his annual Holy Thursday letter to priests throughout the world. In that letter, he repeated his theme with even greater intensity:

---

[4] *Gift and Mystery, op. cit.*, 75.

[5] *Ibid.*, 77.

May we always celebrate the Holy Eucharist with fervor. May we dwell long and often in adoration before Christ in the Eucharist. May we sit at the "school" of the Eucharist. Through the centuries, countless priests have found in the Eucharist the consolation promised by Jesus on the evening of the Last Supper, the secret to overcoming their solitude, the strength to bear their sufferings, the nourishment to make a new beginning after every discouragement, and the inner energy to bolster their decisions to remain faithful.[6]

Priests are also men who have embraced what John Paul calls the "treasure" of celibacy. His view of the Latin Church's discipline of celibacy is obvious—even in today's world where it has come under such criticism, and many have left, citing the celibate life as their reason for departure. No need to be surprised at such charges—from within or without—the Pope reminded priests in his first Holy Thursday letter in 1979:

Did not Jesus Christ, after He had presented His disciples with the question of the renunciation of marriage for the sake of the kingdom of heaven, add these significant words: "Let anyone accept this who can"?[7]

Even more to the point is why celibacy, in John Paul's view, is a treasure. He refers to Saint Paul's proclamation that each person in the Church has his or her own particular gifts, and celibacy is precisely that, a gift, a "gift of the Spirit":

Celibacy "for the sake of the kingdom" is not only an eschatological sign, it also has great social meaning in the present life, for the service of the People of God. Through his celibacy, the priest becomes the "man for

---

[6] *Letter of His Holiness Pope John Paul II to Priests: Holy Thursday, 2000* (Vatican City: Libreria Editrice Vaticana, 2000), 13.

[7] *Letter of the Supreme Pontiff John Paul II to All Bishops of the Church and to All Priests of the Church* (Boston: Daughters of St. Paul, 1979), 22-23.

others," in a different way from the man who, by binding himself in conjugal union with a woman, also becomes, as husband and father, a "man for others," especially in the radius of his own family.... The priest, by renouncing this fatherhood proper to married men, seeks another fatherhood and, as it were, even another motherhood, recalling the words of the Apostle about the children whom he begets in suffering (Corinthians, Galatians). These are children of his spirit, people entrusted to his solicitude by the Good Shepherd. These people are many, more numerous than an ordinary human family can embrace. The pastoral vocation of priests is great, and the Council teaches that it is universal, it is directed toward the whole Church.[8]

A priestly life must also be one of personal prayer, based on the daily need every priest has to be converted anew. The Holy Father mentions several components of each priest's inner journey. Each is called on to give an account of his heart, his service, his zeal and fidelity to Christ, since each has been entrusted with Christ's mysteries. Also, like all fellow sinners, the priest must account for his own negligence, sins, acts of timidity, lack of faith and hope, and of thinking in only a human way. The priest must seek forgiveness of God over and over again in the Sacrament of Reconciliation, and he must ever realize that prayer is the first and last condition for conversion, for spiritual progress and for holiness of life.

In John Paul's view, then, the priest, this man uniquely configured to Christ, this man of the Eucharist who has embraced the treasure of celibacy and the life of prayer has accepted a unique and very demanding vocation. Yet our Holy Father is just as quick to remind priests that they do not carry their burden alone; the Lord carries it with them. His thoughts seem singularly appropriate today when the demands are so great, and the results often times disappointing. It is the opinion of his bi-

---

[8] *Ibid.*, 24.

ographer George Weigel that John Paul has made a tremendous impact on the present and future priesthood, not by merely "breathing new life into an ancient idea—the priest as *alter Christus*," but also because, by his own personal example, he has "given young men a challenge to heroism that many have found compelling."[9]

It is not simply that John Paul offers timeless thoughts in the contemporary age, he also has addressed very specifically what it means to be a priest in these times. When he celebrated his golden jubilee in 1996, he had admitted how much the world had changed since his own priestly ordination. There were new challenges, new problems, new lifestyles, and the contemporary culture of the late twentieth century differed greatly from the post war world of 1946. This did not mean, though, that the priest of today is to be a different sort of man from the priest of 1946:

> Certainly the priest, together with the whole Church, is part of the times in which he lives; he needs to be attentive and sympathetic, but also critical and watchful with regard to historical developments. The Council has pointed to the possibility and need for an authentic renewal, in complete fidelity to the word of God and tradition. But I am convinced that a priest, committed as he is to this necessary pastoral renewal, should at the same time have no fear of being "behind the times," because the human "today" of every priest is included in the "today" of Christ the Redeemer. For every priest, in every age, the greatest task is each day to discover his own priestly "today" in the "today" of Christ to which the Letter to the Hebrews refers. This "today" of Christ is immersed in the whole of history— in the past and future of the world, of every human being and of every priest. "Jesus Christ is the same yesterday, today and forever" (Hebrews 13:8). If we immerse our human and priestly "today" in the "to-

---

[9] George Weigel, *Witness to Hope* (New York: Harper Collins, 1999), 658.

day" of Jesus Christ, there is no danger that we will become out of date, belonging to "yesterday." Christ is the measure of every age. In His divine, human and priestly "today," the conflict between traditionalism and progressivism—once so hotly debated—finds its ultimate resolution.[10]

Whether one speaks of the contemporary priesthood of the twenty-first century, or any other period of the Church's life, it makes little difference: the priesthood is the priesthood. John Paul assumes certain givens, especially what a priestly vocation is:

It is the fruit of an inexpressible dialogue between God and human beings, between the love of God who calls and the freedom of individuals who lovingly respond to Him.[11]

Karol Wojtyla's response differed greatly from those who have been raised in the culture and affluence of the West. His life was set against the background of the Second World War: his nation lost some six million of its citizens, killed in combat or murdered; Auschwitz loomed ominously in the national psyche; and after the war Poland was occupied by the Soviet army. In addition, Wojtyla's own family witnessed great hardship: his mother died when the future Pope was only a boy; his brother, a medical doctor, died at a young age; and finally his father, with whom he shared lodgings as a young man, died suddenly—all before Karol's twenty-first birthday. He would reflect on that inner illumination to be a priest, which became stronger as the years passed, and was deeply influenced by his father's example of prayer and sacrifice, a "domestic seminary," as he called it. The priest raised in today's culture would have little, if any, appreciation for such hardship. Yet, as John Paul

---

[10] *Gift and Mystery, op. cit.,* 83-84.
[11] *Pastores Dabo Vobis, op. cit.,* 61.

notes, it is today's culture the priest finds himself in, and in which he must work for others, while at the same time working out his own salvation. This was very much in the Holy Father's mind as he wrote *Pastores Dabo Vobis*; he took his theme and title from the book of the prophet Jeremiah. Faced with seemingly insurmountable problems, Jeremiah began to question his vocation, and felt frustrated and disillusioned because so much of his preaching was falling on deaf ears—not at all unlike the culture of the twenty-first century. Just as there was an innate human hunger for truth in Jeremiah's time, so our Holy Father sees a corresponding hunger for Christ in our times; he sees it as the one expectation contemporary men and women have of priests. "Every other need—economic, social and political, can be met by any number of other people. But from the priest, they expect Christ, and they have the right to receive Christ."[12] How do contemporary men and women receive Christ through the Church's priests? In the same ways they always did, through the Eucharist and the sacrament of Reconciliation:

> The priest has a mysterious, awesome power over the Eucharistic body of Christ. By reason of this power he becomes the steward of the greatest treasure of the Redemption, for he gives people the Redeemer in person. Celebrating the Eucharist is the most sublime and the most sacred function of every priest. As for me, from the very first years of my priesthood, the celebration of the Eucharist has been not only my most sacred duty, but above all, my soul's deepest need.[13]

Our Holy Father's words here are reminiscent of an American cardinal's statement that the Eucharist, the Blessed Sacrament, is the *raison d'être* of the priesthood, and the observation of an American bishop that any young man considering a priestly vocation would be more than willing to give his life for a mystery, but never for a question mark.

---

[12] *Gift and Mystery*, op. cit., 85.

[13] *Ibid.*, 85-86.

Not only is the priest the human instrument bringing the Lord's Body and Blood to the faithful, but he also, in the name and person of Christ, has the power to forgive sin—to bring Christ's reconciling love, peace and strength to others. "It is in the confessional," the Pope writes, "that his spiritual fatherhood is realized in the fullest way."[14] If he is to be an effective confessor, however, the priest must make frequent use of the Sacrament of Penance himself, going often, and receiving regular spiritual direction.

Throughout his life, Karol Wojtyla has taken the Sacrament of Penance very seriously. It is the tribunal of mercy where one's sins are forgiven, and where the penitent receives a special sacramental grace which strengthens one's inner resolve. It is also, for him, an exchange of ideas between two individuals where one comes to know the truth and live it. The goal of confession is the sanctification of all life. By taking in life in all its dimensions, looking at the person I am, the person I could be, my vocational clarity might be brought into sharper focus.

The contemporary priest is also called to be a man of the word, to proclaim the word, and most especially to live by the word. At the same time, the Holy Father is convinced that he must be a man intellectually prepared to know the word in depth, and to proclaim it effectively. Our days are marked by a high degree of specialization in many areas. As a result, intellectual formation is extremely important, as is ongoing theological formation. Such formation makes it possible to engage in serious dialogue with the contemporary culture. Therefore, each priest is called upon to know far more than an extensive list of doctrinal truths and definitions; he must be able to explain those truths in detail, geared to those he is sent to serve, and made applicable to their lives and individual circumstances.

Whether our Holy Father is speaking of the priesthood in general or of what it means to be a priest in today's world, he always includes what he calls the "Marian thread." In his book

---

14 *Ibid.*, 86.

Gift and Mystery, his thoughts go back to the Carmelite monastery in his native town of Wadowice, where he received the scapular of Our Lady of Mount Carmel, and where his earliest Marian devotion began to develop. As a young man living in Cracow, he joined a "living rosary" group in a Salesian parish. He has said that since childhood, he was convinced Mary leads us to Christ; in his mature years he became equally convinced Christ leads us to His mother. Saint Louis de Montfort had an enormous influence on his development, since his Mariological thought is rooted in the mystery of the Trinity, and in the truth of the Incarnation. He came to understand why the Church says the Angelus three times a day, and that in it is contained the deepest reality of the greatest event ever to take place in human history. Even his episcopal motto, *Totus Tuus*, comes from the writings of de Montfort.

In his first Holy Thursday letter as Pope in 1979, he bequeathed to all his brother priests that which had so formed him:

> The beloved disciple who, as one of the Twelve, had heard in the Upper Room the words, "Do this in memory of Me," was given by Christ on the Cross to His mother with the words, "Behold your son." The man who on Holy Thursday received the power to celebrate the Holy Eucharist was, by these words of the dying Redeemer, given to His mother as her "son." All of us, therefore, who receive that same power through priestly ordination have, in a certain sense, a prior right to see her as our mother. And so I desire that all of you, together with me, should find in Mary, the mother of our priesthood which we have received from Christ. I also desire that you should entrust your priesthood to her in a special way.[15]

---

[15] *Letter of the Supreme Pontiff, op. cit.*, 31.

12

The Blessed Virgin Mary and the Priesthood

In 1989, John Cardinal O'Connor spoke very candidly to the priests of New York on the subject of vocations:

> In my judgment, nothing advances vocations as does devotion of priests to the Eucharist and to Mary: I don't know that any statistical studies have been done, but from what I observe, those dioceses in which Perpetual Adoration is widespread, personal Eucharistic worship on the part of priests is habitual, and devotions to Our Lady are highlighted—those are the dioceses in which vocations flourish. Vocations aside, however, I am sure you will agree with me that commitment to Our Lord in the Blessed Sacrament and to Mary, Mother of Priests, is as strong a lifeline as any priest could hold on to. I know how much I need that lifeline.[1]

The Fathers of the Church were among the earliest writers to concentrate at great length on Our Blessed Mother. It is difficult to describe the enthusiasm with which they write. One almost feels scholarly objectivity has been set aside to allow the sentiments flowing from the depths of their hearts to be made known. This does not diminish the validity of their writing; it accentuates their strong faith and devotion to the Mother of God. The reason for the Fathers' boundless love of the Virgin

---

[1] John Cardinal O'Connor, *Always a Priest, Always Present* (New York: Archdiocese of New York, 1989), 49.

was answered by at least one spiritual writer who noted the mystery to be found in most believers' relationship to Our Lady. No matter what the particulars of life, no matter how hopeless one's situation may appear, she provides that glimmer of light, that one ray of hope that each soul may cling to. The ray of hope is, of course, her closeness to her Divine Son, and her ability to intercede, in motherly fashion, for all who invoke her. The life of every priest must be inserted into this larger picture; as a celibate man who does not have the closeness of wife and family, his relationship to her takes on tremendous importance; as "another Christ," her motherhood to one configured to her Son is very different from her spiritual motherhood of the faithful. There is not a priest who has not known the sentiments of discouragement or despair so common to humanity, nor is there a priest who does not share in Christ's priesthood as much as his brothers. Hence, a priestly love of Our Lady is inseparable from love of the Son she bore. In short, there is no follower of Christ for whom love of Our Lady is unimportant:

> We are all sinners, and priests are no exception to this rule. ("If we say we have no sin, we deceive ourselves, and the truth is not in us," 1 John 1:8). If we keep this fact constantly in mind, we shall mistrust our own strength, for we shall realize how weak we are. And then we shall never refuse the Blessed Virgin's help, just as a child who is unsure of himself allows his mother to support him when he is learning to walk. We know that she is the advocate and help of sinners, and thus it should never occur to us to ignore her in our pastoral ministry, where our object is precisely to reconcile sinners with the Father. We know that "we go to Jesus—and we 'return' to Him through Mary" or, as Saint Bernard wrote, "For if man fell through a woman, through a woman he will rise." We rise again only through her.[2]

---

[2]   Federico Suarez, *About Being a Priest* (Princeton, NJ: Scepter, 1996), 211.

In his *Summa Theologiae*, Saint Thomas Aquinas speaks of the predestination of Christ to be humanity's Savior, as well as the predestination of humanity's being saved by Christ. Our Blessed Mother, singularly privileged though she was, was completely a creature, and as a creature, predestined to be saved by the Divine Child she bore. She was totally Christ's, and Christ was totally His Father's. Hence, all who love God through His Son, must love the mother of the Son. The point can be made that in bringing humanity to Christ, her intercession can lead all to see more clearly her role in God's plan of salvation.

That plan unfolded in Christ, the second Adam. It is true He could have become incarnate in a fashion similar to that of the first Adam, but as one spiritual writer has pointed out, this might have made Him a model for humanity, but would not have made Him a son of its race. In fact, He was born of an Immaculate Virgin; through her, His priesthood was really formed, because in her He joined His divine nature to a human one. The blood flowing in His veins, He took from her, the blood flowing from His Sacred Heart, in a very real sense, He took from her Immaculate Heart. She who gave the world its Redeemer stood by His cross in total cooperation and love as He offered the one perfect sacrifice of His life for the world's redemption; in the same way she stands with every priest configured to her Divine Son as he, *in persona Christi*, makes that same drama present in every Mass.

Mary might easily be called the Mother of Priests, since she is the mother of Him from whom their priesthood derives. Not only that, Our Lord entrusted His mother to the care of John, the beloved disciple, who stood in for each of us. Mary is, therefore, the universal mother of all humanity, not by a figure of speech, but by the command of her Son. All of us were spiritually begotten at Calvary; priests, then, can claim Our Lady's spiritual motherhood in two ways. Finally, the story continues beyond Calvary. Spiritual writers often note the presence of the Blessed Mother with the Apostles, awaiting the coming of the Holy Spirit upon the Church. Her prayers, they tell us, were directed to her Son, specifically for those men He had chosen and appointed to spread His Gospel. Because of the closeness of Mary to her Son during His earthly life and the salvific events of His death and resurrection, and also because of her closeness to the Church at its inception, the theology of the priesthood has always emphasized that the call of each priest has its origins in the merits of Christ and His Blessed Mother. It might best be described as a response to both their prayers:

> It is Mary who even now unceasingly requests all the graces which we need to persevere in the love of Christ and of souls; to walk in the narrow way of perfection, which is usually against our inclinations; to be zealous ministers; to celebrate each Mass with more fervor than the preceding one. Finally, it is she who will pray for us and who will assist us at the hour of our death. In every instance, we can truly say that Mary prays for us, that she obtains graces for us and influences us spiritually. The Blessed Virgin Mary, from the heights of heaven, clearly sees in our soul the indelible character of Christ and knows with a divine knowledge the mission which every one of us must carry out as priests of Christ. She knows that Our Lord had decreed that He will be represented on earth by men who carry His priesthood in their spiritual being.[3]

The Blessed Mother's role at Calvary was singularly unique. She did not share in the physical sufferings of her Son; rather, she made a self-offering of victimal love. The bond of physical and spiritual affinity between Mother and Son was of such depth that no other human being could understand it, much less penetrate it. Mary was the only spectator at the foot of the cross who really understood all the events in the life of Our Lord, how His very Incarnation had this culmination as its

---

[3]   Pierre Paul Cardinal Philippe, O.P., *The Virgin Mary and the Priesthood* (New York: Alba House, 1993), 21.

purpose. If Christ is the divine bridegroom, and the Church, His mystical body is His spouse, Mary may be said to exemplify the spousal relationship to Christ far more than any creature. As such, she plays a vital role in the interior spiritual life of any priest; she who penetrated the interior depths of her divine Son may, by God's grace, so penetrate the hearts of those who share that Son's priestly life.

Mary at the foot of the cross has been described as the queen who stands beside the king, the mother of the High Priest who shares in every priestly prayer the Son utters to His Father. Saint Albert the Great had this description of it:

> The Blessed Virgin Mary was not chosen by the Lord to be a "minister," but to be the "spouse," that "help" according to what is stated in the Book of Genesis: "Let us make him a helpmate" (2:18). The Blessed Virgin is not a "vicar" [an agent], but a "coadjutrix" and a "companion," participating in the kingdom as she had participated in the Passion, when all the ministers and disciples had run away and she alone remained at the foot of the cross. The wounds which Christ received in His body, Mary felt in her heart.[4]

The priest who makes present the reality of Christ's death in every Mass may, in his human imperfection, not always realize Mary's presence; yet she is uniting herself with every celebrant as he offers in an unbloody fashion, Christ's shedding of His blood for the world's salvation. In trying to explain the beauty of this very mysterious reality, the Sulpician, Jean Jacques Olier, described the intimacy existing between Saint John and the Blessed Mother during the crucifixion:

> Saint John was for Mary the continuation of Jesus Christ... and in the culminating moment of his minis-

---

[4] Cited in *Ibid.*, 54.

try, he was entirely hers. He had to enter into her intentions and lose his own intentions in those of Mary's. He was given to her as her own special priest, so as to offer up the sacrifice for the intentions she wished.[5]

Still another aspect of the relationship between mother and son is discovered in the thought that each priest, in bringing Calvary to bear on the present moment, reproduces the mystery of affection, love and consolation which reached its highest degree of perfection in the Lord's agony and death: that rapture of hearts truly present in every Mass. Our Holy Father, Pope John Paul II has written on this theme, and Cardinal Philippe sums up the Pope's thoughts:

> He was given the power to reproduce the very actions of the High Priest. Moreover, the priestly grace permits him to live the life of a priest as "another Christ." Then, so to speak, the point of departure of the love of the priest for Our Lady is Christ. He loves her as the Lord loved her when He was here on earth, thereby reliving and perpetuating across the centuries the union of Jesus and Mary. It is a love friendship which is truly pure and holy (cf. John Paul II, August 8, 1982). When a priest understands this, his entire life changes. He loves Mary with a pure and distinct love. He loves her with a strong and vital love. In the hour of isolation, or perhaps of temptation, he sees in her the secure friend whom his human heart desperately needs. The Immaculate Heart of Mary is the heart that the priest needs so that "he may not feel alone."[6]

The late Archbishop Fulton J. Sheen had much the same in mind when he developed a meditation on every priest's relation to Our Lady. In a beautiful comparison, Sheen notes that

---

[5] M. Olier, *Le Vie Interieure de la Très Sainte Vierge* (Paris: 1875), cited in *Ibid.*, 76.
[6] *Ibid.*, 77-78.

each priest gives up the earthly love of a woman, and Mary gave up the earthly love of a man. Every priest has freely surrendered himself to Christ at his ordination, and his surrender is not unlike that of Our Blessed Mother; she willed her Son and she conceived. The priest willed to be God's (he can often identify the day and the hour with precision). The more he gives himself to that surrender, the more he realizes that only those who have truly given themselves to Christ can be free. Our Blessed Mother knew, Archbishop Sheen pointed out, that there could be no conception without fire and passion, and that was the working, the overshadowing of the Holy Spirit within her. In like manner, the priest cannot live without a similar fire and passion, that of "intensified spiritual love." If there is to be a "generation of souls," if a priest is to be a "father begetting souls," the Archbishop said, there must be the same fire and passion of the Holy Spirit overshadowing him. As in Mary, virginity and motherhood were united, so in every priest, virginity and fatherhood must take root. This is not the absence of love, it is rather the "fullness or ecstasy of love":

> As Mary's spiritual motherhood was not a privilege apart from humanity, so neither is the spiritual fatherhood of the priest. Nothing so provokes the service of others, as a sense of one's unworthiness when visited by the grace of God. Mary, hastening over the hills in the Visitation, reveals how she, the handmaid of the Lord, became the handmaid of Elizabeth. She is now the example of the priest that the Christ within him must prompt dedication to "all those who are our friends in the common faith" (Titus 3:15), and to all mankind. As Mary's visit sanctified John the Baptist, so the visit of the priest-victim will always sanctify souls. Every sick call of the priest will be to him the mystery of the Visitation all over again. Carrying the Blessed Sacrament to his breast, in auto or on foot, makes him another Mary carrying the cloistered Christ within her pure body. No delays on sick calls, no tar-

rying while the family worries, but like Mary, the priest "hastens"—for nothing demands speed as much as the needs of others.[7]

The priest is also called to have a deep love of Mary, not only in his better moments, but even in his failings. He trusts in her intercession to combat his weakness, realizing that no matter what mistakes he has made in his priestly life, the one who has fallen most, the one who had gone furthest off the straight path, will receive the greatest proportion of the mother's love. The way in which the priest is to do this does not differ greatly from the way any weak individual would do it—he has recourse to Mary through prayer and meditation. Prayer, in this instance, especially means the recitation of his daily Rosary. Decades ago, in a retreat conference to priests, Blessed Columba Marmion stressed the importance of this powerful lifeline to heaven in the daily spirituality of priests:

> Now, why is the Rosary so efficacious? First of all, on account of the sublimity of the prayers which make it up. The *Pater* comes to us directly from the love and sanctity of the eternal Father by the lips of His Son Jesus; the *Ave* was brought down from heaven with the salutation of the angel Gabriel. The Church, as the interpreter of the needs of her children, has added a petition to this salutation: she makes us repeat to Mary one hundred and fifty times the request that she may be with us now and at the hour of our death. Could there be any request more opportune, even for the priest? Then again, the recitation of the Rosary makes us re-live the different stages of the Redemption. I have said it already, but it is not out of place to repeat it here, that each event in the life of Christ gives forth, as it were, a divine power, and this power operates on us

---

7   Fulton J. Sheen, *The Priest Is Not His Own* (New York: McGraw Hill Book Company, Inc., 1963), 271.

when we meditate on the scenes of the Gospel. Through the Rosary, we render to the Savior, by the mediation of Mary, the worship of our thought and of our love, in His childhood, in His suffering, and in His glory, and in virtue of this contact of faith many divine aids are accorded to us. Besides, in the action of the Virgin, all so simple and at the same time so generous, we find many examples of virtues to imitate, many inspirations of hope, of charity, and of joy.[8]

In the 1940's and 50's, Monsignor Ronald A. Knox, Catholic chaplain at Oxford, and prominent British convert to the faith, was at the height of his popularity as a retreat master, and especially a preacher of priests' retreats in England. In one such course of spiritual exercises, he developed Old Testament characters and themes, showing the parallel between them and the spiritual life of the twentieth century. His treatment of Our Blessed Mother found comparisons in the Book of Esther, but is remembered more for a unique meditation from the *Salve Regina*, or Hail Holy Queen. In each of its phrases were to be found wisdom and insight.

In the Hail Holy Queen, we first invoke Our Lady as *Mother of Mercy*, a title which is reminiscent of the tenderness and compassion we naturally associate with her person. It was a compassion Christ showed to all whom He encountered, a compassion He took from her, a compassion every priest should pray to her to cultivate in his daily life. His is a sacramental life which exudes the supernatural, and all those activities derive from Christ who was born of Mary; his is also a life like so many others, in which darkness often obscures light, and sadness overtakes tranquility of soul; a life in which fear of the unknown, and fear of events beyond death can weaken faith—for all these reasons she is for all priests, *our life, our sweetness and our hope.*

---

[8]   Dom Columba Marmion, O.S.B., *Christ—The Ideal of the Priest* (London: Sands & Co. Publishers, Ltd., 1952), 300.

Turn then, most gracious advocate, thine eyes of mercy towards us might best be prayed by the priest as he reflects on Mary next to her Son on Calvary, and next to each priest as he makes Calvary present in the Mass. Monsignor Knox makes the point that Mary's gaze at her crucified Son and all the injustice perpetrated against Him does not for a moment preclude a downward gaze at the many crucifixions and injustices in human lives, and a final upward gaze of intercession for all who have recourse to her, who won countless merits for us by her sharing her Son's Calvary on earth, and to whom we pray *after this our exile, show unto us the blessed fruit of thy womb, Jesus.*[9]

Mary it is, then, who prays for every one of her priests, so that their priesthood may be fruitful. She obtains for them enlightenment and help, things which we would never have had if she had not interceded for us. She bears toward each priest a special role which is proper to her because of her maternal role; she teaches each priest how to be a good father of souls. Mary it is who gives each priest a tremendous amount of compassion for those who suffer and especially for those who are weak. She gives us a spirit of sacrifice which allows us to spend ourselves in service to others, and a spirit of prayerfulness which allows us to live our lives in close communion with the eternal High Priest. She reminds each priest that she lived on earth the same life of faith in the Son of God, which he is called upon to live. She teaches every priest to entrust his priesthood to her maternal protection, and to pray incessantly, *O clement, O loving, O sweet Virgin Mary.*

---

[9]   Ronald Knox, *A Retreat for Priests* (London: Sheed & Ward, 1946), 176-177.

Bibliography

Abbott, Walter J., S.J. (ed.), *The Documents of Vatican II*. New York: Herder and Herder, 1966.

Code of Canon Law, Washington: Canon Law Society of America, 1983.

Directory for the Life and Ministry of Priests, Vatican City: Libreria Editrice Vaticana, 1994.

Dolan, Timothy M., *Priests for the Third Millennium*, Huntington, Indiana: Our Sunday Visitor, Inc., 2000.

Dulles, Avery Cardinal, S.J., *The Priestly Office*, New York: Paulist Press, 1997.

Dunn, Patrick J., *Priesthood*, New York: Alba House, 1990.

Farrell, Walter, O.P., *My Way of Life*, Brooklyn: Confraternity of the Precious Blood, 1952.

For Love Alone: Reflections on Priestly Celibacy, Middlegreen, Slough: SAINT PAULS, 1993.

Galot, Jean, S.J., *Theology of the Priesthood*, San Francisco: Ignatius Press, 1985.

Garrigou-Lagrange, R., O.P., *The Priest in Union with Christ*, Cork: The Mercier Press Limited, 1951.

Harvey, Francis P., S.S., *Retreat Companion for Priests*, Rockford, Illinois: TAN Books and Publishers, Inc., 1950.

Hume, Basil Cardinal, O.S.B., *Light in the Lord*, Middlegreen, Slough: SAINT PAULS Publications, 1991.

Knox, Ronald A., *A Retreat for Priests*, London: Sheed & Ward, 1958.

_____. *The Priestly Life*, New York: Sheed & Ward, 1958.

Manning, Henry Edward Cardinal, *The Eternal Priesthood*, London: Burns and Oates Limited, Undated.

Marmion, Dom Columba, O.S.B., *Christ—The Ideal of the Priest*, London: Sands & Co. (Publishers) Ltd., 1952.

McGovern, Thomas J., *Priestly Identity*, Dublin: Four Courts Press, 2002.

Nichols, Aidan, O.P., *Holy Order*, Dublin: Veritas, 1990.

O'Connor, John Cardinal, *Always a Priest, Always Present*, New York: Archdiocese of New York, 1989.

Pennington, M. Basil, O.C.S.O., and Rev. Carl J. Arico, *Living Our Priesthood Today*, Huntington, Indiana: Our Sunday Visitor, Inc., 1987.

Philippe, Pierre Paul Cardinal, *The Virgin Mary and the Priesthood*, New York: Alba House, 1983.

Pope John Paul II, *A Priest Forever*, Athlone: SAINT PAULS Publications, 1984.

_____. *Gift and Mystery*, New York: Doubleday, 1996.

_____. *Letter of His Holiness Pope John Paul II to Priests, Holy Thursday, 2000*, Vatican City: Libreria Editrice Vaticana, 2000.

_____. *I Will Give You Shepherds: Pastores Dabo Vobis*. Boston: Pauline Books and Media, 1992.

_____. *Letter of the Supreme Pontiff Pope John Paul II To All the Bishops of the Church On the Mystery and Worship of the Holy Eucharist*, London: Catholic Truth Society, 1980.

_____. *Letter of the Supreme Pontiff Pope John Paul II To All the Bishops of the Church and To All the Priests of the Church On the Occasion of Holy Thursday, 1979*. Boston: St. Paul Editions, 1979.

Ratzinger, Joseph Cardinal, *Ministers of Your Joy*, Middlegreen, Slough: ST PAULS Publications, 1989.

Rutler, George W., *The Cure d'Ars Today*, San Francisco: Ignatius Press, 1988.

Sheen, Fulton J., *The Priest Is Not His Own*, New York: McGraw-Hill Book Company, Inc., 1963.

_____. *Those Mysterious Priests*, Garden City, New York: Doubleday, 1974.

Socias, James P. (Comp.), *Priesthood in the Third Millennium: Addresses of Pope John Paul II: 1993*, Chicago: Midwest Theological Forum, 1994.

Suarez, Federico, *About Being a Priest*, Princeton: Scepter Publishers, Inc., 1996.

Suhard, Emmanuel Cardinal, *Priests Among Men*, New York: Integrity, 1949.

The Catholic Priesthood: Papal Documents from Pius X to Pius XII, Dublin: M.H. Gill and Son Ltd., 1957.

Trochu, François, *Curé d'Ars: A Biography of St. Jean-Marie Vianney*, Manila: Sing-Tala Publishers, Inc., 1998.

Vanhoye, Albert, S.J., *Our Priest is Christ*, Rome: Pontifical Biblical Institute, 1977.

Van Zeller, Dom Hubert, O.S.B., *The Gospel Priesthood*, New York: Sheed and Ward, 1956.

Weigel, George, *Witness To Hope*, New York: Harper Collins Publishers, Inc., 1999.

ST PAULS

This book was produced by St. Pauls/Alba House, the Society of St. Paul, an international religious congregation of priests and brothers dedicated to serving the Church through the communications media.

For information regarding this and associated ministries of the Pauline Family of Congregations, write to the Vocation Director, Society of St. Paul, P.O. Box 189, 9531 Akron-Canfield Road, Canfield, Ohio 44406-0189. Phone (330) 702-0359; or E-mail: spvocationoffice@aol.com or check our internet site, www.albahouse.org